Poems, Original, Lyrical, and Satirical, Containing Indian Reminiscences of the Late Sir Toby Rendrag – Primary Source Edition

Toby Rendrag

POEMS.

POEMS,

ORIGINAL, LYRICAL, AND SATIRICAL,

CONTAINING

Indian Reminiscences

OF THE LATE

SIR TOBY RENDRAG, M.N.S.

―――

" *Quæ ad omnes pertinent,*
" *Ab omnibus debent tractari.*"

―――

LONDON:

PUBLISHED BY W. BOYLS,

WEYMOUTH-STREET, PORTLAND-PLACE.

AND BY

GEORGE EAST,

HANOVER PLACE, REGENT'S PARK.

――

1829.

J. GAMBLE,
Printer, Mortlake, Surry.

CONTENTS.

—◆—

CONTENTS.

PREFACE.

The late Sir Toby was for many years resident in India, and a keen observer of Asiatic men and manners.

After his sudden demise, his papers (from among which the following are extracted) fell into my hands, as one of the Executors. Among them were discovered some extraordinary morceaus, bordering on originality of style. What follows, may for the present suffice as a specimen; by Indian readers they will be fully understood.

Whether my late friend ever intended them for publication is a question, which the hand of death now forbids my positively deciding on, though I am inclined to believe he had an *itching* that way, and although a perpendicular, straight-forward man, seldom verging to the right or left, still he would appear to have had misgivings, as to how *his lucubrations* might be received, if ushered into print before an English public, who knew little, and cared perhaps still less, about India.

All that need be added is, that his sketches and ideas of Indian society are by no means over-drawn, and that thousands now in existence, can bear testimony to their general fidelity.

A few of the notes have been added since his death, and I trust the selection, though for particular reasons, divested in the *present edition*, of his most *piquant morceaus*, and entirely devoid of political matter, will not prove of any detriment to the memory of my late much valued, and worthy friend Sir Toby.—" Peace to his manes, may the sod lay light upon his ashes."

INTRODUCTION.

——— " Ridiculum acri
" Fortius et melius plerumque secat res."

My name is Toby—and I do not care—
I have no wish to purchase any other;
My father had no words (good man) to spare,
So left the matter to his wife my mother,
Who sought our *pedigree*—a test to try us,
And dubb'd me " *darling, little,* dear *Tobias !*"

I went to school to try my A, B, C,
The master found the boy loved cake and play-things,
My father *mum* ('twas best), my mother she
Vow'd that *her son** should never want for gay things;
So when she thought I had enough of knowledge,
I got a tutor, and was enter'd College.

* My dear mother claimed me entirely as *her own,* and would
never permit father's interference. The good man's maxim was—
" Well, any thing for a quiet life."

B

Enough—no more—description here must close—
Of *self* no more—('tis meet to the discerning)
But just to tell we had a *brazen nose,*
Or " John Bull" lion, on our door of learning,
And as *Mama's** own maid said I had *genus,*
I, in *poetics,* told her she was - - - - Venus!

If you would write love verses—(by the way
I give you this as kind of " *introduction*")
Call not a woman young, if she be *grey,*
Her mirror else may question the production.
Let reason be your guide if prone to flattery,
Though few I own are proof 'gainst such a battery.

Some marvel how it is—but it is so—
Females of *certain years* don't talk of ages—
And one or two, it is my luck to know,
Who *Time's* unmannerly, grey wrinkled rages,
Would treat with scorn—yet 'tis *I think* romancing
When long past *fifty*—to ape girls in dancing.

---

* As some *young* ladies of *forty,* or upwards, speak of their
Papas and *Mamas,* I hope the privilege may not be denied to poor
Toby!

Disgusting some might think, and say with truth—
To view ag'd matrons *girlish* manners aping,
Affecting all the airs of romping youth,
For admiration still on tip-toe gaping;
And then a lisp—as if proud fond *Mama*,
Had still been living with *dear good Papa*.

Both dead, perhaps, full thirty years or more—
Yet *poor Mama* has something youthful in it—
An anecdote of *old times* is a bore—
An old acquaintance dropp'd should he begin it ;*
Age hath its follies—her's the most deplorable,
Who, old and ugly, would be still adorable !

Each mortal man or woman is too prone,
To view with partial eyes a near relation—
They see each other's foibles as their own,
Unless they quarrel—then, all's degradation !
Since cruel facts proclaim, what nature smothers,
No foes are more inveterate than *brothers !*

* So it is " Truth should not be spoken at all times." I know
an old acquaintance who was shunned by an *old* lady, for obtruding
an anecdote, which had occurred to them thirty years preceding—
poor man, your loss was *little*.

B 2

Good gentle reader, pardon what is here—
I'm no bluff personage of *grim* morality;
" *Toby*" may sometimes range o'er subjects *queer*,
But won't detain you long, with stale formality;
If morals *stupify* the daily papers
No wonder our gay ladies get the *vapours*.

My neighbours have a right to know 'bout me,
Because I have a wish to know my neighbours;
I hope, like neighbours, we'll not disagree,
But jog in peace at our respective labours.
This world's a world of care, of woe, and joy,
" Per tot discrimina rerum"—here am I !—

Yes ! *here am I*—and sad may cry ALACK !*
For many a day before I see old Britain—
What mistress " *Fate*" has hidden in her *pack*,
I hope in golden letters big is written.
The sea wave rolls—a storm—'tis dark and windy,
And Fate ordains that I must rhyme in *Indy*.†

---

* *Alack !* This word, in the Hindoostanee language, signifies one hundred thousand.

† Meaning the " *India Gazette*," in which this first appeared *in print*.

PREFACE TO CALCUTTA.

"Cum tristibus severe; cum remissis, jucunde."

READER, if you're disposed to take a joke,
And relish *Pagets*,* or such modish smoking,
Just try a pipe—whilst I a smile provoke,
Laughing is vulgar—and might end by choking—
Grin if you please, an idle hour beguiling,
Lord Chesterfield permits the use of smiling.

Perhaps, you'll say stale verse is grown a bore,
Since Paley's days no logic or no moral.
Think what you please, I'll never feel it sore,
Nor forge a pin whereon to hang a quarrel.
In numbers smooth, dear maidens, let us jog,
Concise as *Southey*—elegant as *Hogg!*

* A small silver pipe, with a bowl at the bottom to hold water for the smoke to pass through: brought into vogue in Calcutta by Sir Edward Paget.

Some, may have heard, or seen what here is written,
Some, ne'er about strange customs teaze their heads;
I little care if none of them are bitten
By Hindoo morals, or *Byragee** beads.
Too long a residence in foreign parts
May change our habits, and contract our hearts.

Books are the essence of all useful knowledge,
But observation join'd to common sense
Does more for mankind than the lore of College:
'Tis seeing—mixing—gives us just pretence
To what Ascetics still are for abolishing,
A knowledge of the world, and its polishing.

Right thinking certainly is gain'd by travel;
Our Saint Helena ladies once agreed
(Nor could they otherwise the thought unravel)
That London must be very dull indeed!
Since all the fleet of China ships that day
Had with two frigates anchor'd in the Bay.†

---

* A sect of Hindoo mendicants, many of whom travel the country over. Some Europeans, from a long residence in India, become almost Hindoos in habit.

† The anecdote was related to me of a Saint Helena lady having

I mean no disrespect to Saint Helena ;
But only just exemplify what is
The case with many, who have never seen a
Foreign station, or outlandish phiz :
Who cannot stomach flying bugs, and fishes,
Long-winged foxes, or fig-leaves for dishes.

Many there are, not Saint Helena ladies,
With strange ideas form'd of foreign parts,
Who stare; and giggle at whatever shade is
New to their eye—with *La's !* and other starts*—
Ready to burst their tittering sides asunder,
Till use, and reason, fly away with wonder !

If ignorance be bliss, as poets rhyme it,
What fool for wisdom then abroad would roam ;
One's native land is far the sweetest climate,
So Saint Helena people relish home.

expressed her concern, for the dull state London would be in during
the absence of half a dozen China ships, and two men of war. The
natives of Saint Helena are called " yam stocks," a *polite* term, to
designate them from the European part.
    * The reader, doubtless, has seen many such.

They've *quite enough* of hill and dale variety,*
And when a fleet comes in, what's *called* society !

Yes, Saint Helena ! rock amidst the ocean,
NAPOLEON's ashes spread far fame to thee :
He who changed empires—kingdoms put in motion,
The Hero to whom monarchs bent the knee.
Beneath three freestone slabs,† and willows green,
Low rests the greatest man this world has seen.

Steep is the valley—drown'd by mountain shade,
And pure the spring that flows beside his pillow,
Green grows the sod—unknown to plough or spade,
Geraniums flourish, crown'd by weeping willow.
Here silence reigns—as if in mute contrition,
Whilst Glory seems to wail for dire ambition.

The world has had enough of gore, and glory,
Of Alexander, Cæsar, Greece, and Rome,

---

* Saint Helena is evidently a volcanic eruption—nothing but ups
and downs—hill and dale ; yet the natives, I am told, rarely wish
to quit their uneven rock.

† Three plain freestone slabs, without any inscription, taken
from the kitchen floor of his new house.

Of Troy's famed conquerors in ancient story,
And now of him, who met an early doom.
Sequester'd here his ashes lone may lie,*
Not so his *fame*—for glory cannot die !

Such glory—no ! "Renown" the task be *thine*,
To paint to future states, and distant ages,
A Hero doom'd by Victory to shine
A star in History's most lasting pages.
Marengo ! Lodi ! who can thee forget ?
Thy sun, too, Austerlitz ! can never set.

Yet, Fortune press'd *too far*, may one day turn,
With double power retrograde her way.
Genius for fame and victory may burn,
But what was *Buonaparte* 'gainst Fortune's sway !
There are, who think 'twere well—I think so too—
Had his heart's blood been spent *at Waterloo !*

* The feelings of the Gentlemen who accompanied me to view
the tomb of Buonaparte at Saint Helena, were evidently excited—
especially when standing on the freestone slabs which covered his
body : we looked at the slab, then at each other—and departed in
solemn silence : an indescribable feeling of solemn awe came over
us, and we left the spot meditating on the inscrutable power and
dispensations of the Almighty Disposer of mankind.

Now, " gentle reader,"* prithee be polite,
And don't look dainty as if forc'd to swallow
Thin airy notions—some may deem them trite—
I little care, if dulness does not follow.
Should critics condescend their castigation,
Let justice reign, without exaggeration.

Thus much by way of *preface* to my " sketching ;"
I write to please my reader—*not for pay.*
If any think too far I have been stretching,
I'll hear with patience—but must answer *nay !*
Should valued judgments *dub* my verse a *bore,*
I can't help rhyming—but can PRINT NO MORE !

* This is a term which I hope to find I have *justly* used, and
which I have taken the liberty to borrow from Henry Fielding, and
some others.

CALCUTTA.

" If you would make a speech, or write one,
" Or cause some artist to indite one,
" Don't think, because 'tis understood
" By men of sense, 'tis therefore good;
" But let your words so well be plann'd,
" That blockheads can't misunderstand."

I.

GENIUS of RHYME! alas, too often bought,

I can't address thee well, till cooler weather—

In this, plain prose will scarce afford a thought,

Much less a chime that sense would tack together.

If thou wouldst verify thy itching power,

Oh! bribe me with a cooling thunder shower.*

II.

Great Laureat of our Isle! what gain'd THEE bays?

A pipe of malmsey too at thy command—

* When this sketch was commenced the thermometer stood at
98, the atmosphere excessively close and hot.

Some style thy verses wild, some puny lays,
Some Brobdignags, that none can understand.
Was it " Kehama's Curse,"* with Hindoo seers,
Dull longs and shorts, and flying Glendoveers ?

III.

Quaff thou thy malmsey—*beer* must do for me—
I'm no one's poet—but the Muses' *odd* son :†
Let but the air I breathe be cool and free,
With inspiration pure, and clear as *Hodgson*.‡
Whilst witlings on Pegasus prance, and *rat too*,§
I sing CALCUTTA, perch'd upon a *Tattoo !*‖

* Respect for England's Laureat elect, forbids further comment.

† " *Odd* son." This phrase may be taken literally, or " ad libitum" as the reader pleases.

‡ The inspiration here alluded to, is not to Mr. Hodgson himself; but to Mr. Hodgson's *beer*, which is by far the best, and most sought after in India, and goes under the name of " *Hodgson*." In Calcutta " Hodgson" sold for 50 per cent. more than Meux, Whitbread, Barclay, or any other brewer. Indeed, no *fashionable* would let any other "*go down*" but " Hodgson !"

§ Poets sometimes *rat*—as well as M. P.'s—barring offence to any Honorable Member.

‖ " *Tattoo*" is the Indian name for a small low-valued pony.

IV.

Sketches! yes, sketches, Sir, you need not stare,
They're merely sketches fit for rainy weather—
Of Dons, streets, houses—pick'd up " here and there,"
Fantastically caught, and thrown together.
I picture no one—but if any trace it,
My answer is " *Qui capit ille facit.*"

V.

Excuse my Latin, which was meant for prose,
For sober " Sketch Books," not poetic sketches:
May huge musquittoes* tickle that man's nose,
Who to his neighbour any portrait stretches.
Since " *Veluti in Speculum,*" 's a maxim known,
Let every honest fellow TAKE HIS OWN.

VI.

There are, perhaps, who think 'twould be as well,
Whilst I'm about it, to apologize

---

* Strangers, on their arrival in India, find these insects, which
differ in size, particularly troublesome. Calcutta and its environs
in particular. Some hundred miles up the country there are very
few musquittoes. They prevail most towards the end of the rainy
season, and among jungles and swamps.

To *Indian* readers, for long notes which swell
A duodecem to octavo size.
Few English readers know Hindoo phraseology—
So much by way of preface, and apology.

VII.

Calcutta! I have seen thee—and what then ?
Beheld thy *great house,** gobbling cranes, and stables—
White, black, fat, tawny, big and little men,
Turks, Jews, Armenians, Arabs, ships, and cables—
Sepoys, and shady walks, near Chaudpaul-Ghaut,
Fort William, which at foe ne'er fired a shot.

VIII.

'Tis not the worse, I'll tell you though, for that,
And so will any *Baboo, Dutt,* or *Sunkur*†—

---

* The Government House. These are the first objects observed by a stranger on landing, especially the Government House, with the long-legged Indian cranes (called Adjutants, from their measured strides) perched on the top of it. These birds are not permitted to be molested, as they devour dead dogs, cats, filth, snakes, and indeed every thing they can master. I have seen one gulp six or seven young ducks for breakfast, and he was about to serve the mother the same trick, but was prevented by the servants running just in time. Chaudpaul-Ghaut, here noticed, is the principal landing-place. There is a shady walk between it and Fort William.

† These are terms of rank and cast among Hindoos.

In all *Tiretta's** market there's no flat,
No *Khansaman,*† no *Kidmutgarish* skulker,
No *Shroff* in Burrah, or in Lall Bazar,
Would vote Fort William thundering in war !

IX.

I know a little of the *Baboo*‡ race—
I know *Sircars* have little love of glory ;
Unless that glory rests in golden peace,
And " Master's favour," or a gainful story—

* " *Tiretta's* Bazar," or market, is a large enclosed square, built by a Portuguese gentleman of that name, and the best, bad as it is, of which Calcutta yet can boast.

† A *Khansaman*, is a head butler, who takes charge of all plate, dinner apparatus, &c. purchasing the various eatables, and cheating as much as he can. A *Kidmutgar* is an attendant at table under the Khansaman, whose place he sometimes supplies. In Calcutta they are very knavish. A " *Shroff*" is a native banker, or money broker. " *Burrah*, and *Lall* Bazar," literally signify great and red market.

‡ A *Baboo* is generally understood to be a Hindoo of wealth, either in or out of business, and is a kind of title annexed to people of consideration; but not quite so common as our Esquire. *Sircars* are people employed to " *do business*," keeping accounts, purchasing articles, &c. They have generally an eye more to their own business than to " Master's," though all they profess to covet is " *Master's favour*." Some of these, by *honest* industry, and " Master's favour" become rich " Baboos!"

'Bout Honor's " *ways and means*" not over nice,
Provided, aught's to *gain* in shape of *Pice !**

X.

They're sometimes friendly—and with clack, and pother,
Chime most devotedly, when gain's the bent—
Like hounds, they'll hunt in concert with each other,
Nor " come to fault" so long as gold's the scent.
Keen search of lucre, 'tis my firm opinion,
Rules their *lost* souls,† with autocrat dominion !

XI.

Our Hindoos are a wary, cautious people,
Sly, graceful in deportment, seldom rude—
Like Musselmans their temples have no steeple,
They worship *Ram*‡ for money, and for food.

* The current copper coin are Pice, four of which make one Anna, and sixteen Annas one Rupee.

† "*Lost souls*," alluding to what some of our *liberal*-minded Missionaries preach to the natives of India, by way of convincing them of the benefits and charity of Christianity, that they must inevitably *go to hell!*

‡ "*Ram*" is the principal Hindoo deity—and "*Ram Ram*" a common term of salutation between Hindoos of cast. As to elegance of manner and address, there are no people more soft, plausible, and insinuating than Hindoo gentlemen of education, who have mixed with the world. Some of them beat Lord Chesterfield hollow!

Though slow to anger, and averse to borrow,
They always have an eye for what's to-morrow.

XII.

Not so your Musselmans—they're lewd, and proud,
Viewing with inward scorn as vile deceivers
All other sects—they raise their voices loud,
Abusing when they dare all unbelievers.
Like Spanish Priests, they'd plunder, purge, and vomit,
Jews, Pagans, Christians—for their saint *Mahomet!*

XIII.

Some reader here may think that bile or spleen
Hath led me from the path of true narration:
I talk as I have heard, read, known, and seen
All Musselmans are foes to toleration.
To gain their favour free from sneers, derision—
Let grow your beard, and then try - - - *circumcision !*

XIV.

Waving religion, be it understood,
That Musselmans are liberal, bold, and zealous;

c

Careless of money, prodigal of blood,
Obliging, neighbourly, when not too jealous.*
Fond of their ease, wit, wine, and jocularity,
They sometimes court like us, for popularity.

XV.

Upon this subject we have said enough ;
Besides " *Qui hiis*"† may think it stale or foolish :
Still worse—the Muse seems rather in a huff
Like some fond Miss in love, grown sick and mulish.
" Proceed (she says) you've other theme to handle,
" Or I will leave you, and your farthing candle."

XVI.

" City of Palaces !"‡ I greet thee low,
Although I think the term inapplicable—

---

* This is the natural consequence of their wives being concealed
from the eyes of mankind, and their not being stinted to one.

† The literal meaning of " *Qui hii*" is " who's there?" Old Bengal residents have obtained the appellation, from using it so frequently to their servants—as have the European residents at Madras the name of *Mulls*, from their liking to Mulligatawny soup ;
and at Bombay " Ducks," from the use of a fish nick-named " Bombay Duck." These fish, when dried, eat well with rice, and I
knew an old gentleman, who, after his return to Europe, had kept
a sample of them for sixteen years, to put him in mind of " olden
times !"

‡ This appellation to Calcutta is grander sounding than true—

There's vanity enough, God knows, and show;
But *palaces* may suit an Eastern fable!
Some houses are substantial, airy, roomy,
And others dirty, mean, close, hot, and gloomy!

XVII.

Calcutta! low, I greet thy modern walls,
Thy drains, rails, tanks, straw huts of Hindoo labour,
Large, straggling, flat-roof'd houses, good for squalls,
Scarce one in shape or size like to its neighbour.
Improve thy streets, lanes, bridges, rails and pottery,
Nor waste the public money gain'd by Lottery.*

near a large good-looking house, mean straw sheds and huts are frequently erected, so that both grandeur and poverty strike your visual optics at the same time. No symmetry or regularity.

* A six monthly Lottery has been established for many years past, *"for the improvement of the city of Calcutta,"* which, including certain Town duties, ought to yield several hundred thousand Rupees annually. Much was done in the government of Lord Hastings for this "City of Palaces," but much still remains to be performed for its beauty and salubrity. The native and denser part of it requires treble its present ground to stand on, and all the poor matted and mud huts of this "*City of Palaces*" should be placed in a situation by themselves. Where new streets are to be built, some degree of uniformity should be observed. The Calcutta pottery alluded to, is the best in Bengal, or on that side of India, and famed for its porous quality, and coolness in keeping water.

XVIII.

'Tis true, thy buildings *some* are worth a viewing—
Yet, sober Hindoos pass them one and all,
To see thy " *Great House*," and what's there a doing,
Scarce deigning one side glance at yon Town-hall.
Long may'st thou hold thy proud exalted station,
" *Great House*"* of fame—the wonder of each nation !

XIX.

Thy lions rampant, and thy kingly arms,
Thy double fronts, and wings in circle winding,
Thy stuccoed domes, and marble halls have charms,
When dust, hot winds, and Hackery wheels† are grinding,
Compar'd with *thee*, I've never seen thy brother—
I wish *our King* (poor man) had *such another.*

XX.

Fair is the strand‡ from asses, cows, and pigs,
And gay the scene at eve on ev'ry Sunday;

* " *Great house.*" This is the name given to the Government House, in contradistinction, no doubt, to *little* house.

† " *Hackery wheels.*" A Hackery is supported on two wheels, and is drawn by bullocks—it somewhat resembles a rough, ill-constructed Irish car. As to the Government House, it is a suitable residence for any Emperor or King. Part of this magnificent building was intended by Marquis Wellesley for public offices.

‡ " *The strand.*" This is one of the greatest improvements that

There half-cast Dandies* drive their loves in gigs,

And debtors (one in seven) have no *dun* day.

Flags, masts, ships, sinnaces, here far surpass

The roaring beach—vain-glory of Madras!

XXI.

Try not our city eastward here too far,

Where narrow zig zags† give poor natives shelter;

Where many a drunken *Dhobie*, and *Lascar*,‡

Fight, dance, and fiddle—tumble helter skelter;

Where Methodistic fanatics§ may snarl

At laughing Hindoos, perch'd upon a barrel.

has yet been made to this city. The drive at present along the banks of the river, which would in breadth contain four coaches abreast, is about two miles, and will be extended. There, ships of different nations, from eight or nine hundred tons burthen, down to the smallest boat that skims this rapid stream, are to be seen floating majestically at anchor, or close alongside of the different wharfs. Their flags on Sundays are very gay.

* "*Half-cast Dandies.*" Gentry half European and half native, some of whom *would be* the tip-top of Exquisites! Oh, Vanity! Vanity! thou art not confined to any rank, skin, or colour.

† "*Zig zags.*" There is no want of these in Calcutta. One lane, in particular, is called " Zig Zag Lane!"

‡ "*Dhobie* and *Lascar*." The first is a washerman—the latter, a native sailor.

§ "*Fanatics.*" Some who *call themselves* " reverend," with zeal bordering on fanaticism, have been seen to mount a barrel in a

XXII.

I never fancied vagrant preachers' canting,
Illiberal on all subjects but long prayers ;
Vulgar, illiterate—stretching truth by ranting
'Gainst worldly cravings, and grim Satan's snares.
Such as I've met, liv'd well themselves and thriving,
With flocks of children—for they all love wiving.*

XXIII.

In modes and manners, there's a wrong and right
And so there is in spiritual instruction ;

public market-place, and there hold forth, in true *ranting* style, against heathens and their religion—whilst the Hindoos treated their abusive epithets, some with ridicule, but generally with silent forbearance and contempt.... This is not the way to convert—better *such* apostles would stay at home. Many years' experience leads me to be of the Abbe Dubois' opinion generally. At all events, education must be the ground work, and hundreds of years, if not thousands, pass away, before Christianity gains thorough footing in India.

* "*Wiving.*" Yes, our missionaries in India always take care to provide themselves with nice, pretty, agreeable helpmates, comfortable houses, and other good things of this life. It has been my fate to fall in with *some* of these people, whose zeal was not confined to the natives—but annoyed the company which chance led them into, by opinions and assumption founded on ignorance of the natives of India, equally uncharitable and unchristian. The more ignorant, the more bigotted were these men in their illiberal and unjust aspersions.

The fear of hell may heathen minds affright,
But education bears a sure production.
No Missionary serves a cause religious
By speech offensive, ranting, and litigious.

XXIV.

Stray not too far past that Bazar called Bow,
'Mongst dirty lanes of Chinese, swine, and nailers;
Butchers, and grog-shops, clothes arrang'd for show,
And courtezans you'll meet, with drunken sailors.
Bidding adieu to each vile lane and grunter,
I like the Town-hall, lighted up, by Gunter.*

XXV.

Its architecture is a clumsy piece—
It is not Roman, that's my plain opinion;

---

* Mr. Gunter, here noticed, is the major-domo, and manager of all balls and feasts given in the Town-hall. For some years the gentry were afraid to dance in the ball-room above stairs, lest the house should tumble—but the experiment has latterly been tried without much risk; and confidence to "the light fantastic toe" completely restored. Mr. Gunter is an excellent caterer; and I believe a near relation of Gunter, who figures in the same line in London.

Nor is it Moorish—nor yet much of Greece—
Old *Vanburgh's** style might fairly claim dominion.
View'd from the road bold swells its front, and doughty,
With shapeless pillars, like legs swoll'n, and gouty.

XXVI.

Here, feasts are held—here, Champaign cool doth flow—
Here, City wits spout flaming long addresses;
Here, new arrivals *come* in hopes to *go*,†
Flirt, ogle, dance—then lisp forth their distresses.
" Hotter than Bath rooms these—you've seen the upper—
" I fear Mama won't let us stay for supper !"

* *" Vanburgh's style."* The best elucidation of Sir John Vanburgh's style, is his epitaph by Pope :

> " Lie heavy on him earth, for he
> " Laid many a heavy load on thee!"

† *" New arrivals."* So are called young ladies *fresh* from Europe. After the arrival of ships from England, a common question among the Calcutta dames, is—" Have you yet seen the new arrivals ?" The first place where the new arrivals are generally to be met with, is taking " a fashionable airing" on the race course. Their roseate complexion easily distinguishes them from such, as a longer residence in this baneful climate have turned to the lily—mais n'importe !

XXVII.

Near this famed Hall stands Court yclep'd " *Supreme*,"*
Fenc'd from the public gaze by iron railing;
Where many a briefless lawyer *sat* to dream,
On fees to come—his luckless bag bewailing.
Sore disappointments often forc'd to smother,
A large retainer's given—but to *another !*

XXVIII.

I cannot say I ever lov'd the law,
Although *some* lawyers are, I know, good fellows;
And in indictments sometimes find a flaw,
To save an honest brother from the gallows.
I've met one (after talking dead a sinner)†
In a grand jury room, quite *mum at dinner*.

XXIX.

Good laws were made to keep in check bad men,
And Lord knows there's no use for any—"*but* a"—

---

* This Court is so styled from it's acting independently of the Government, and its judges being appointed by the Crown. The building itself has nothing grand about it : it is among the oldest public structures in Calcutta. Some of the barristers, I fear, find the time hang heavy. Competitors are becoming numerous, and the *golden age* is in its wane in every department.

† "*Talking dead a sinner*"—the unfortunate man was hanged.

I've seen large cities, more than nine or ten,
But no police so bad, as in *Calcutta.*
If magistrates *be fit* to fill their station,
I blame the *climate then, for relaxation.**

XXX.

In London to get drunk is thought a crime,
But in Calcutta it is no such evil;
Police-men here (*good Sirs,* excuse the rhyme)
Care not for magistracy, or the D——l !
One league maintains their gain, their cast, their houses—
They care for money only, and their spouses.

XXXI.

I do not say *their spouses rule the roast,*
For with our Hindoos there is no such matter;

* What every one says must be true, and every one agrees that the Calcutta police is its disgrace. Men who are fitted by activity and capacity to fulfil the station of magistrate should be appointed by the Supreme Court, to whom they should be responsible. Or, perhaps, a preferable method might be, for the citizens of the higher class to elect a mayor and magistrates, subject to the authority of the judges. At present, the patronage rests solely with the Governor. As Calcutta increases in size, the present system must change. Anno 1824.

Unlike good English wives, 'tis true, they boast
Of dress, and jewels—sit cross-legg'd and chatter—
Yet, when their wedded lords but shew their faces,
They run like rabbits to their hiding places.

XXXII.

I know a reason I could tell for that,
'Tis no where to be found in Coke, or Blackstone—
Mahomud was not fond of ladies' *chat*,
Nor did old Menu,* patronize their *clackstone*.
Their laws, however wise, had ne'er been written,
Had they beheld the lovely dames of Britain.

XXXIII.

Our Eastern nobles seem like other folks,
Fond of their ease, good eating, smoking, drinking;

* *"Menu."* The famed lawgiver of the Hindoos. Neither he
nor the Mussulman Prophet appears to have placed much confidence
or respect in the opinions and conversation of females. *Clackstone*
is a word, which, although not to be found in Johnson, carries its
meaning with it. As both Mussulman and Hindoo ladies receive
no kind of education but just to please their lords, and as very few
of them can read or write, it cannot be supposed they are much
fitted to combat any idea or opinion with the wise men of the East;

At meals, like us, they sometimes cut stale jokes,
But seldom speak on subjects without thinking.
Mahomud's sons are one and all notorious
For belching, jealousy, and lives uxorious.

XXXIV.

Calcutta Baboos are a portly race,*
Gain is their idol—pastime, pain, and labour ;
In manner complaisant, demure in face,
Ready to overreach a friend, or neighbour :
To compass ends (just as the maggot seizes)
They'll speak, think, act, and even sham diseases :

* *"Portly race."* When Hindoos become rich, it is necessary
they should become fat ; for which purpose they consume an extra
quantity of clarified butter called Ghee—and resort to every other
likely method of obtaining a proper rotundity : to be rich and lean
is not at all lucky, or becoming, in the idea of a Hindoo ; and as
Baboos are comfortable people before they obtain that title, to see
a *lean* Baboo is rather an extraordinary spectacle.

In this place it is requisite to notice, that to eruct wind, is not
thought by any means indecorous or ill-bred among Musselmans or
Hindoos ; on the contrary, it is esteemed by some as a polished
ease of manner—and, snapping their fingers, they return God
thanks for the deliverance.

XXXV.

Life a fam'd Pope* (the story's good for metre)
Who had a dreadful stoop until he found
What he'd been looking for, the keys of Peter—
Head shaking, body bent, and bandag'd round—
But when the keys he got, surpris'd the cardinals,
By stature fresh, and straight, dress'd in their farthingales.

XXXVI.

Mistake me not, nor think this too severe,
Doubtless there's honour to be found among some;
Some, in professions too have prov'd sincere,
And wicked consciences *perhaps* have stung some.
Some deal forth charity—and all agree
All young Hindoos love *nautching,*† and *all* old ones *Ghee!*

* "*Fam'd Pope.*" The story is related of the famous pope
Sextus the Fifth. Cardinals in those days used to dress in a sort
of farthingale, or ruff. It is told of this Pope, that, previous to his
election, he assumed all the appearance of a man worn down by
age, and on the brink of the grave; but the day after his election,
to the dismay of the Cardinals, he appeared quite upright and vi-
gorous.

† "*Nautching.*" This word means *dancing,* of which young
Hindoos like to be spectators. Dancing women sing, and usually
keep time to the music with little bells fastened to their ankles. At

XXXVII.

My object's not to be morosely witty,
No *tender* feeling willingly I'd shock.
Return we, then, to view this rising city,
St. John's Cathedral, and St. Andrew's cock*—
A brazen cock, to view the Hooghly flowing,
And Doctor B——ce would have it gilt, and crowing.

XXXVIII.

Of public buildings there are eight or ten,
Cathedral, Kirks, and Chapels nearly twenty ;†

grand marriages and public festivals, such as the " *Doorgah Poo-jah*," this *nautching* is maintained in great style, and Europeans are invited. The word " *Ghee*," clarified butter, has been explained before for the benefit of the European reader. It is used both for eating and softening the skin by rubbing.

* " *St. Andrew's cock*." This cock surmounts the spire of the Scottish Kirk, chosen it is said as an appropriate emblem by its reverend pastor, between whom, and the late Bishop Middleton, report says a difference arose about the erection of a spire; and *vulgar* people will have it, that the cock perched aloft, and in the act of crowing, represents *victory!* *If it be so*, the sentiment certainly is not one dictated by the meek spirit of Christian humility and forbearance.

† " *Twenty*." It is impossible with the plan of this work to enter into a description of each public building, even were they worthy of the trouble. " St. John's Cathedral" and " St. Andrew's Kirk" have both tolerable organs, as has what is called the " Mis-

Exchange, and play-houses all open, when
Actors and audience can be found in plenty.,
Shops, auctions, long rooms, and repositories,
News' rooms for scandal—libraries for stories.

XXXIX.

Those days are gone, when strangers might have found
A house, a bed, a friend, a welcome hearty ;
Now hospitality, alas ! is bound
To shew off plate, at some stiff dinner party.
Calcutta now may boast of state formality,
Without one decent inn,* in its locality.

sion Church." There are Armenian and Greek churches, Methodist and Portuguese chapels, Jewish synagogue, Mosques, &c. &c.
As to places of amusement, they are but few : two theatres, badly
supported—two large auction rooms—repositories for horses—news'
rooms, &c.

* "*Decent inn.*" Much to the inconvenience and annoyance of
strangers there is not one "*decent inn*" or "*hotel*" in all Calcutta ;
—and as to hospitality, those days are gone by. Thirty years ago
it was different, and a different race then inhabited this city : but a
continual influx of strangers, and its increasing size, has shut the
doors of most, except to their immediate connexions. To add to
the difficulties of a stranger in Calcutta, no furnished lodgings are
to be had, and letters of introduction are not paid the same attention to as formerly.

XL.

For loungers to pass time a *little gaily*,
There's Tulloh's auction, and there's Leyburn's too;
At one or other, there's a horse sale daily,
Where you'll meet people who have nought to do.
Members of boards, collectors, secretaries—
Captains, cadets, clerks, and apothecaries.

XLI.

In days of yore (I need not tell the years).
Calcutta belles and beaux would often ramble.
To see gay long rooms,* and hear auctioneers,
Dring, Williams, Hohler, Roworth, Gould and Campbell.
Worthies who in their day expert could pull a
Bow, just as neat, as Leyburn can, or Tulloh.

XLII.

'Tis fair to draw an ornamental bow,
To please dull bidders by a fine oration;

---

* "*Long rooms.*" Dring's long room, in days of yore, was a fashionable lounge for both ladies and gentlemen—many temptations, such as jewellery, plate, &c. were there to be found. The names here noticed had once *their* day; but the iron hand of Death has closed their mouths for ever. Leyburn and Tulloh have now *their* day.

To raise the spirits when a cup too low,
E'en Premiers practise on a drooping nation.
Ye Town-hall Orators !* forbear your sneering,
'Tis no small art—the art of auctioneering.

XLIII.

And there's an art, a *golden art* in puffing,
A knack which failing trade need ne'er disclose;
Snuff void of ornament, is not worth snuffing—
Fine names should tickle ears, as well as nose:
No " *bon vivant,*" who daily thrice must cram,
Without a *puff*, could relish ham, or jam.

XLIV.

Pengelly, Mortimer, and Co.† are wits,
I seldom peep at *Indy's* lucubrations ;

---

* " *Town-hall orators.*" Certain gentry, who think the Almighty
has been kind to them, spout hacknied orations, upon hacknied
themes, in votes for addresses to a governor, a commander-in-chief,
or member of council. No sooner is it known for certain, that a
governor or commander-in-chief is to depart for Europe, than a
meeting is convened at the " Town-hall" to prepare an " *Address.*"

And then doth genius rare, in language fine,
With gaudiest tropes and figures proudly shine !

† This is a famous house for puffing, and for witty attempts, as
columns of the India Gazette might serve to shew, had I not mis-

But *whole* anchovies set me into fits,
Of sore mouth-waterings, and such perturbations.
Come, Madam Muse, if you'd have sense and metre,
Add *Carbonell,* well iced,†* far better than *saltpetre.*

XLV.

Wit and true humour seldom fail to please,
Yet, in hot weather one can scarce be merry ;
There's no bad joke in ham, or Stilton cheese,
Wash'd down with *Simpkin,‡* or fine sparkling perry.
If this idea you agree in, go
And try the WIT of Pengelly and Co. !

XLVI.

If for variety your taste doth hanker,
You'll suit all wishes in Calcutta shops ;

laid them.   One I recollect was recommending customers to eat the
anchovies—" not the bottles !"   However, these good people spared
neither the puff oblique, nor the puff direct, and I hope their wit
has not been puffed in vain.

* Carbonell's claret is much esteemed in India.

† *" Iced."*   When there is no ice, saltpetre is used for cooling
wine or water : indeed, saltpetre is in general use, ice being rather
a scarce article in India, and a great luxury.

‡ *" Simpkin."*   A word used by the natives for champagne.

Where you buy needles, you may find an anchor,

Or Yorkshire hams, beer, broad cloth, hats, and tops :

But if in quest of French or foreign goods,

Try whistling W—shire,* first of blue-skin bloods.

XLVII.

Others there are who keep more splendid shops,

Rich jewellers—spruce milliners—and coach-makers ;

Confectioners deal here in mutton chops,

And wig-makers are sometimes undertakers.

Trades of all kinds, and wits you'll light upon ;

But poor *Kit Dexter*†—he is dead and gone !

---

* "*Whistling W—shire.*" This person kept a shop in Calcutta, which he has now relinquished—having it is to be hoped acquired a fortune. He used to fall a whistling when people came into his shop, with a careless air, and by this *musical* manner disgusted many—the most conceited half-cast perhaps in all India.

† "*Poor Kit Dexter.*" Christopher Dexter was known as a wag, an honest, but eccentric character—he had pursued many avocations, and at last died in Calcutta a wig-maker, I believe, about the year 1822. There is a story related of him, that being on a jury where a gentleman was tried for manslaughter, he took a *quantum sufficit* of bread and cheese in his pocket to enable him to hold out against the other jurors, as he was of opinion "no gentleman should suffer for only killing a black fellow."

XLVIII.

No disrespect is meant to other wits,

Whose names (however worthy) meet no mention;

I have a value for Calcutta Cits,

And slight to any 's far from my intention.

Should any feel neglect, 'tis my petition,

They'll send their names and wits, for next edition.

XLIX.

'Twere vain to wander o'er Calcutta streets,

Or tell hard names to those who do not know them;

At every turn a stranger always meets

Some keen Ramzanny,* who will gladly shew them.

Each corner's known to every rogue and cully,

From Chitpore road, to Ranymoody gully.†

L.

The native names of streets have great variety

Not like Italian music much, I fear;

* "*Ramzanny.*" A Musselman name, very common for a low servant of all work, or an idle fellow of no work.

† "*Ranymoody gully.*" These are the extremities, not of the whole of Calcutta, but of the denser part of the city.

The aspirates and gutt'rals cause satiety,
Sounding discordant to an English ear.
Judge for yourself, you'll find I am no joker,
Birjeetullāw—Gow Khannāh—and Saumpokhur !

LI.

Chouringhee ! last not least, where all the great
Big-wigs and *secretaires* are found improving
Stale native laws, and resources of state,
(New ones, you know, should keep the old ones moving)
Has courts, and houses fit for Lordly dwellings,
Would hungry jackals cease their midnight yellings.

LII.

Fronting Chouringhee lies that famous course
Where morn and ev'ning drives yield health and pleasure ;
Where *eligibles*† lisp forth soft discourse
To their *intended*—last, though needful measure :

* *Chouringhee."* Although this part of the city lies to the Southward, it might fairly be called the *"West End,"* as all the fashionables, and men of note, *secretaires,* &c. generally reside here. Greater numbers of jackals prowl about Chouringhee at night than in the denser part of Calcutta, and their "midnight yellings" are most unpleasant.

† *"Eligibles."* This signifies a person who has either rank or

Since, howe'er long the Dame has patient tarried,
She must be *Gigg'd** *one week*, before she's married.

LIII.

I mean not here to say that people tarry,
Or court, or think on matrimony *long ;*
To day you see—the next intend to marry—
The third propose—then think if you've done wrong—
The fourth, all's settled, at some party jigging—
The fifth, the *system* you commence of *gigging !*

LIV.

E'en our Eurasians,† if their fortune's ample,
In gig or chariot frequently you see,

income sufficient to make him a desirable object for the "*silken noose.*" Civilians are generally "*eligibles:*" as for Ensigns, Lieutenants, or even Captains, few of *them* come within the meaning of the term, and must put up with what they can catch.

* "*Gigg'd.*" The meaning of being *Gigg'd* is to be driven about the course for a week or ten days, previous to entering the silken noose, to the stare and gratulation of an admiring public. Some wits have called this being *carted !*

† "*Eurasians.*" Natives of India, *half* European—so politely termed instead of the plain meaning word "*half-cast.*" Before a marriage actually takes place, the parties betrothed ride out together in a gig, or carriage, for four or five days, sometimes longer

They aim at *fashion*, and a good example;
Before the Priest, or Parson, feels his fee
The lady veils (averse to observation)
To try an airing—and " *talk conversation.*" *

LV.

'Midst all my sketches, and poetic gildings,
I've overlook'd, but let them pardon this,
That sober range ycleped " *Writers' Buildings*" †—
" Never, than later," had been more amiss.

—and then *matters* are looked upon by a "discerning public" as
quite fixed, and *certain*. The term "*Eurasian*" was, I believe,
first *sanctioned* by my Lord Wellesley.

   * " *Talk conversation.*" This is a phrase which has sometimes
been used by our "*Eurasian*" ladies, who like gentlemen to "*talk
conversation.*"

   † " *Writers' Buildings.*" There is a sombre range of buildings
which go under this name—they once looked more respectable than
at present, owing to the great improvement which has been effected
of late years in the surrounding edifices. I am happy, however,
to say, that the extravagance which their unthinking inmates once
practised, has now greatly ceased, if not entirely grown out of fashion. So long as money could be obtained formerly, extravagance
knew no bounds. A friend of mine long since deceased, was obliged
to take the roguish son of a person who had lent him money, as his
Moonshee, or pedagogue—he afterwards made him his *Dewan*, or
minister, and when appointed to the collectorship of a district, was
nearly ruined by the villanous tricks of this native, who left no

Once people here play'd hazard, and the winner
Sported Champagne at Tiffin—Hock at dinner.

LVI.

Those were the days when writers kept a table,
Spruce turban'd menials, and a singing band ;.
Hounds in the kennel—hunters in the stable,
Their salary not great—nor much in hand—
Writers we know don't shake Pagoda trees,
Three hundred was their pay, in mint Rupees..

LVII..

Marvel not, reader, nor distort your brows—
"The *ways* and *means*," young statesmen soon should study—
Expert as Financiers—no *where's,* or how's,
All sun-shine—money came—gay hope gleam'd ruddy.
Affairs when thriving can't be term'd mere "*gloss-overs*"—
Some must have found that stone call'd ' *the Philosopher's.*'

LVIII.

Bright rays of sun-shine cannot always last,
Sircars and Shroffs, as friends, are *sometimes* fickle ;.

stone unturned to get money, and to obtain what his father had lent
one hundred fold: In short, he plundered right and left, and was
at last dismissed with disgrace.

When bills on bills for payment come too fast,
Dame Credit droops her head in ticklish pickle.
"*No money, Master!*" hard the cruel sentence—
But harder still is many a year's repentance.

LIX.

"*Tempora mutantur*"—Horace says is Latin,
And so do we—(don't look so very blue ;)
In all this city's ways I once was pat in,
But time will change old faces into new.
If great's your wish to see a "*burrah Feringhee*,"*
You'll find *that caste* all huddled in Chouringhee.

LX.

Chariots, cow-coaches,† carriage palankeen,
Gigs, curricles, and phaetons, shew off daily ;

---

* "*Burrah Feringhee.*" These words mean a great European,
and may be construed "a great man." I before noticed that *Chouringhee* was the fashionable end of the town.

† "*Cow-coaches.*" There are palankeen carriages (like palankeens) drawn on four wheels, generally by two ponies, or small horses, called *tattoos*—and open coaches for children, with a covering on the top just to keep off the sun, drawn by bullocks. There is no city in the world, perhaps, that shews off a greater variety of vehicles than Calcutta.

Mornings and ev'nings big folks may be seen
Dashing along the course in order gaily;
On horseback, too, you'll meet men tall and busy, *
Beside a great one, on a little pony.*

LXI.

Soon as soft ev'ning's sun has ceas'd to beam
Chariots commence—one drive the repetition—†
Fair ladies here salute those they esteem
With bows, or nods, or smiles of recognition.
Whilst others, when they chance to come together,
Complain of head-ache, nerves, and melting weather.

LXII.

My observation's meant not to disparage,
There's no accounting (wise ones say) for taste;
I say so too—in equipage or carriage,
What one deems needful, others think a waste.

* "*Little pony.*" The Governor General (Lord A.) usually rode
a small grey pony when taking his morning airings, with generally
two gentlemen on each side on large horses.

† "*One drive the repetition.*" The race course is the usual ride
of a morning, and the road to Calcutta from thence; backwards and
forwards, the general evening drive, where all the equipages show
off—and some very good, when not disfigured by dirty servants.
An evening drive here, puts one in mind of the drive in Hyde Park.

Calcutta coaches are not to my mind,
With breechless, dirty *Syces** stuck behind.

LXIII.

As exercise is best obtain'd by motion,
Our office people sometimes mount a hack ;
And gay civilians (as it suits their notion)
Will sometimes dress in white, and sometimes black.
Parsons and lawyers can't escape your knowledge,
Or dandy writers, just let loose from college.

LXIV.

Blue-coated sailors dash along at random,
Cock'd hats, if *lac'd*, don't go so very fast ;
Red coats and caps are met with driving tandem,
And generals you'll know by being last.
Scotia's cadets† fair blooming like their heather,
A staff, or aid-de-camp, by his white feather.‡

* "*Dirty Syces.*" Syces are grooms, who usually run with horses (one to each horse). Some of them are seen clinging like large baboons behind a coach, or landaulet, and in such dirty, unseemly plight, as to disfigure, if not disgrace, the appearance of any carriage.

† "*Scotia's cadets.*" The sons of Scotia greatly preponderate in our eastern hemisphere.

‡ The sense here is to be taken literally—cocked hats with a long white feather, is the established uniform of officers on the staff.

LXV.

It sometimes happens—(facts one need not smother)—
A title gain'd by service, wounds, or wit,
Descends by death unto a younger brother,
Alike for honours or for rank unfit.
Exalted rank's not always the concomitant
Of wit, or wisdom—nature stands predominant.

LXVI.

I could be if I chose somewhat ill-natur'd,
The muse is willing—but that's not my plan ;
What though a man or woman's born hard featur'd,
The faults of nature one should lightly scan,
Unless the owner had 'midst other failings
A crooked manner, in his worldly dealings !

LXVII.

Some men do credit to their situations,
Some, well are bred—and some I know not what ;
Some, utterly unequal to their stations :
Sense, wit, or breeding, is not sold or bought.
Bad as the jest of knaves, or fools the scoff is,
More grating still is a vain " *Jack in office.*"

LXVIII.

Such as I've known, by routine, chance, and bowing,
Ascend to office—void of all pretence
To any depth—dame Nature scarce allowing
A threadbare stock of plodding,* common sense.
Well might indulgent friends with wonder stare,
To think what magic wand could place *him* there!

LXIX.

Fortune's a lottery—and I'll maintain it—
Some loll in silks—some tramp in cotton rags;
Interest breeds fame†—how few have luck to gain it,
In India ev'ry Scotsman finds his legs.
I do not mean to say they'd run away;
Oh, no! the sun there shines—and they " *make hay !*"

---

* "*Plodding.*" Such is very often the case—that plodding, mere
accident, or routine, has elevated a man to fortune, whilst others, of
far superior ability and merit, remain unnoticed and unknown.

† "*Interest breeds fame.*" How many are there, who, wanting
interest, have wanted opportunity to acquire laurels, and how
many who have had honours and laurels almost thrust upon them:
nor are there a few who have deserved reward, and remain, through
want of favour, unregarded and neglected.

LXX.

There is a quality—(a very good one)
To aid each other is a sign of grace ;
But there's a rule—a golden understood one—
"*Provided* always" you're from the *right place*—
I think the place may safely lie between
The "Firth o' Forth," as far as *Aberdeen !*

LXXI.

Most Scotsmen have a quality adhesive
In foreign parts I've heard—though *not at home*—
To aid each other they use arts persuasive,
And hand-in-hand will round the wide world roam.
So in Calcutta, as in other parts,
When *Scot* meets *Scot*—they've friendly flowing hearts.

LXXII.

I've never found that others were so *clannish,**
Nor for each other often thought or cared—

---

* "*Clannish.*" The word clan is well known, and is still thought
of with regard, by our northern Scots when "*far frae hame !*" Instead, however, as deserving reproach, I deem this a quality which
controls many a baser passion, and sets forth the national feeling
of a warm and an honest heart.

An Englishman cares not if you are Spanish,
French, Dutch, or Irish, so that he be spared
The trouble of knowing who, and what you are;
Your bus'ness, country, be it near, or far!

LXXIII.

For different objects different bosoms burn—
Gain, health, wealth, honours, happiness, variety—
Good and bad taste, are met at every turn :
Much show—small comfort—congealate society:
'Midst all this city's grand and costly pageants,
The people who thrive best, I think, are—"*Agents!*"

LXXIV.

Some to the top of agency ascend
In such great hurry as to cause a dizziness—
Unmindful of the merits of a friend,
"So teaz'd," so "worried," by a "*press of business.*"
Sundays yield leisure—gardens some explore,
Or visit the wild beasts at Barrackpore.*

* "*Barrackpore.*" Barrackpore is fourteen miles from Calcutta. Here there is a large military cantonment on the banks of the Hooghly, and a fine country-seat and park of the Governor General. In this park, where are fine walks and rides, are kept several

LXXV.

Yet, pure sound agency is in it's wane,
Banks are the source of all fictitious credit;
"Too much of sun-shine often ends in rain"—
An useful truth—and fearlessly I'll spread it.
Some by their notes* in luxury may revel;
But money, like the sea, will find it's level.

LXXVI.

If habit's nature—why should we expect
From men of bus'ness more than shrewd plain dealing;

species of wild beasts and birds, in houses built for the purpose. Ostriches, cassiowaries, swans, ducks, &c. are suffered to go at large, and have reservoirs of water for their use. Lest the word "*Agent*" be not fully understood by the English reader in its oriental acceptation, it may be noticed, that he is the same as a Banker in England, but on a more extended scale—giving interest for money lodged with him, and lending that money at superior interest, or perhaps trading with it in different ways, incurring, of course, all the responsibility. Hence have arisen the many losses and failures that have taken place in Calcutta—and, on the other hand, the immense fortunes that have been realized by some *Agents* in a very few years. Most of the Agents have "*garden houses*" two or three miles from Calcutta, to which they retire for relaxation on Sundays.

* "*Notes*." At this writing (1824) there are no less than four Banks in Calcutta, which inundate the country and town with their notes—the sight of hard cash is rare, and, for any amount, almost become a curiosity.

Yet, some there are, who common rules neglect,

Fair—open—candid—high in liberal feeling.

Find me the agent generous—'tis but rarely—

In half a century, you may meet a FAIRLIE !*

LXXVII.

Refin'd ideas do not always follow

In trade's dull track—nor is it meet they should;

Else one poor man might beat another hollow,

And take for evil, what is now call'd good.

Trade has at all times various claims upon her,

And men in bus'ness different views of honour.

* *"Fairlie."* William Fairlie. I have taken the liberty to mention this gentleman's name (who is now no more) as an example of all that is honourable, just, and liberal, and the Prince of Indian Agents. Many is the man's fortune he was instrumental in making. There is an anecdote related, that in the year 1799, when money was extremely scarce in Calcutta, and the Marquis Wellesley could not at the moment speedily raise it, for the charges of the war against Tippoo Sultan, that William Fairlie, by his single name, raised in one day more than half a million sterling from the native Shroffs, or money brokers, in Calcutta, and sent it to the noble Marquis. Such was the esteem and confidence among the natives which the name of *Fairlie* inspired.

E

LXXVIII.

Long may our merchants thrive on sumptuous diet,
May Banks grow fewer for the public weal;
Constituents be pleas'd—and slumber quiet,
Sircars grow honest, nor dread *Burman** steel:
Hard cash, not paper, readily be found
Near the "*Lall Diggee,*"† and its streets around.

LXXIX.

Yes, all around—'Tis time, though, I should notice
Others deserving of a passing line:
If you but knew how very dry my throat is
You'd soothe my song, and ask me home to dine.
Indulgent readers, pardon singularity,
I never had much taste for regularity.

---

* "*Burman steel.*" Some of the *monied notices* of Calcutta did
not at all relish the Burman war, especially at the outset; but the
fictitious credit of Bank paper alluded to, is far more dangerous
than all the Burmans can do.

† "*Lall Diggee.*" This is a famous large tank of the purest and
best water in Calcutta, in the neighbourhood of which are the offices of several Bankers and Agents. A guard of Sepoys, viz. two
sentinels, are placed over it to preserve it from defilement.

LXXX.

I mean a regularity in rhyming,
A studied form of dull, jog-trotting song;
My ear delights in tuneful, easy chiming,
In verses not too short, nor yet too long. ·
With Southey, Wordsworth, *some* might wish to cope;
But give *me* bards like *Byron, Moore,* and *Pope!*

LXXXI.

And yet it's said—good God! what clumsy ears—
What soul, what spirit, could attempt to shew it,
(After a lapse of just one hundred years)
That Alexander *Pope* was *not a poet!*
If *Pope* be not a poet, *who* can claim
A distant title to a poet's name?*

LXXXII.

" *The march of intellect*" may sport its creed,
And deem our ancestors dull mules, or asses;

* It was *attempted* to be shewn, in a number of the "Edinburgh
Review," some years back, that Pope was not a poet.—Quere:
What bard has Scotland ever produced to put in competition with
Pope? If Pope be not a poet, what is to become of *all the Poets-
Laureat* since his time, and of at least fifty more, who far surpassed
these Poets-Laureat.

The world can judge—now most folks write and read,
Adown Time's stream, *Pope's* name triumphant passes.
From the straight track my *Tattoo's* ever stretching,
Pardon I crave, and recommence our sketching.

LXXXIII.

Viewing Calcutta, thus some folks you'll know,
Sircars have keen looks and fine umbrellas—
*Hurkarrahs,** deck'd in turbans made for show—
Sleek *Konsumans,* well fed and brawny fellows:
Pedlars† with books assail you ev'ry day,
And *Coachmen,* roaring out to clear the way!

LXXXIV.

Children you'll meet, if you're an early riser,
By goats or *Tattoos* drawn in solemn state;

---

* "*Hurkarrahs.*" An Hurkarrah may be termed a running foot-
man—they run with palankeens, and are sent on errands, messages,
and with letters, &c. as no such thing as a two-penny post is yet established in Calcutta.

† "*Pedlars.*" Numbers of pedlars perambulate Calcutta with
books, and if any gentleman wishes to form a second-hand library,
he may here soon procure a very good one, at comparatively a trifling expense.

And city clerks, at bus'ness growing wiser,
And *Ayahs** standing at their Master's gate;
Love in their smile (now freed from children's jars)
In amorous converse with spruce *Khidmutgars.*

LXXXV.

A tuft of hair on chin denotes an *Arab,*
A bushy beard, peak'd turban, *Jew* or *Turk*;
The former with a visage worse than carib,
The latter, fit to kill—if not eat—pork.
In wide Panjams, broad turban, you may scan
Patan, Mogul, or *Syud,*† fresh from Hindoostan.

LXXXVI.

Ere *Sol* has risen you hear " *curds* and *whey,*"
And little rice cakes, sold by sound of rattle;
If near Fort William, cannon view you may,
Sepoys with muskets who have seen a battle.

---

* "*Ayahs.*" An Ayah is a nurse, and sometimes serves in the capacity of a lady's maid—many of them delight in intrigue. I have already explained that a Khidmutgar is an attendant at table, and some are great beaux.

† "*Patan, Mogul, or Syud.*" These are sects of the Musselmans, of which, perhaps, many English readers know not there are four different distinctions, viz. *Shekh, Syud, Mogul, Patan.*

Favour'd by wind, on certain roads if blowing,
You'll hear and smell the city dirt-carts* going.

LXXXVII.

If there's a native a fine carriage driving,
With scanty turban—naked,† black, and fat ;
Coachman and horses indicating thriving,
I'd put him down to be a *Baboo* that—
And further, would you seek for native traces,
Half-casts you'll meet, with white hats, and black faces.

LXXXVIII.

Let us ascend a step or two now higher,
Greeks, Portuguese, lean Spaniards—French a few—
Priests I have met, but ne'er a *Nun* or *Friar*—
Chinese with tails and long nails, sharp and blue.

---

* *"City dirt-carts."* These carts often, early of a morning, make a most inharmonious noise, and their effluvia, as you approach, is equally offensive. Their annoyance, however, is guarded against as much as possible by their quitting the city very early. Rice cakes and curds are *rattled* for sale before sun-rise.

† *"Naked, black and fat."* Some of the rich Baboos in Calcutta appear to delight in a scantiness of clothing—disgusting enough, to see a fine equipage, with a naked, black-skinned, fat fellow, lolling in state, greasy and naked to the waist.

Sometimes a *Pontuguese,* or *Spanish Donna,*

Take ev'ning airings near the *Boitaconnah.**

LXXXIX.

Armenians are grave folks and seldom seen,

Black velvet caps portray from whence their race is :

Like us, in bus'ness they are rather keen,

And drive fat ponies at hard trotting paces :

Their wives and daughters† too are very pretty,

With fine dark eyes, fair skin, hair long, and jetty.

XC.

Men of all nations, and all castes are here,

In different places, different trades and manners :

* * *"Boitaconnah."* The Boitaconnah forms part of the Circular
road—which is bounded by what was termed the Mahratta ditch of
Calcutta, in *"olden time."* Here Armenians, Portuguese, Spaniards and half-casts, of all descriptions, may of an evening be seen
driving : in truth, this forms a drive for the sober Cits, whilst the
course is that appropriated to the *fashionables* of Calcutta. As for
Chinese, these consist almost entirely of the lower order, artizans,
shoe-makers, watch-menders, and such-like. Indeed, I never saw
in Calcutta what might be termed a *Chinese gentleman.*

† *"Wives and daughters."* The Armenian ladies are famed in
Calcutta for their beauty, and fine eyes ; but they are very shy, and
seldom or never mix in any society but their own.

Schools, shops, and stables—let by month, or year,
Builders, stone-masons, engineers, and planners.
I cannot enter upon all degrees ;
But all seem eager for what's call'd RUPEES !

XCI.

An Esquire now-a-days is rather common;
There is a story told would come in pat.
I've heard of Tailors—and I know a woman
Might claim the title well*—but "*verbum sat*:"
'Twas formerly annex'd to birth and riches,
Now, ev'ry one's an "*Esquire*" who wears breeches !

XCII.

Of all the places I have ever seen
For *ladies vying*, who will shine and soar most ;
For noisy bull frogs, vanity, and spleen,
Calcutta, we may rank thee far the foremost :

* "*Claim the title well.*" The lady in question I cannot name here—but she has a person, a manner, a visage, a look, and oh! a *tongue*, which might well entitle *her* to breeches, and consequently to the title of *Esquire !*

And when, in days of yore, a *hungry Griffin,*
I thought thee famous, too, for *Pop* and *Tiffin!**

XCIII.

Choice private parties here are seldom full,
In certain groups they meet just as in London :
Calcutta rooms are warm, and *sometimes* dull,
Feasts, routes, and balls, have nearly *some* quite undone—
Servants and Punckas† fill their hot vocation,
Whilst fashion pleads downright for suffocation.

* *"Pop and Tiffin."* "Imperial Pop" is known in England, and in India under the denomination of *"country beer"*—*Tiffin,* to the better informed in England, is known as the Eastern term for *lunch.* The word *"Griffin,"* used here, is a term for a *new comer.* Every person for the first three years after his arrival in India is looked on as a Griffin, or green-horn, from his want of knowledge of the usages, manners, language, &c. of the natives.

† *"Servants and Punckas."* A *Puncka* is a frame of wood, covered with canvass, and ornamented according to taste. Its size is regulated to that of the room where it is suspended from the beams of the ceiling, about six feet from the ground or floor, for the purpose of giving air. It is pulled backwards and forwards by a servant (generally a palankeen bearer) holding a neat cotton rope for the purpose.

XCIV.

Of Indian luxury I've often read,

Yet, seldom has it been my fate to see it :

Victuals enow are on most tables spread,

Often too much—a fault on right side be it ;

But who's to eat ?   Some Indians sit like wizards,

Complaining of stew'd bile, and rotten gizzards !*

XCV.

Livers I should have said ; but lack of rhyme

Has ruin'd many a poet's fine fertility.—

Thanks to the *gizzards*—mine they've sav'd this time,

I'll long remember this, their mark'd civility ;

And if at Cheltenham when they come o'er,

I'll treat them to a glass, *Spa number four*.†

---

* "*Gizzards.*" I hope my old Indian friends will excuse the
liberty here taken with their livers, but the word "*gizzards*" should
not have been used for livers, had not the metre, to correspond with
the sense, *absolutely* required it. May their healths and appetites
bid defiance to hot weather, so as they may relish a sumptuous
dinner, instead of merely *looking at it*, or at each other.

† "*Spa number four.*" When I came home from India the
doctors at Cheltenham set me to drink No. 4. Sherborne Spa; after
a good six weeks' trial, I found that a bottle of good claret, repeat-
ed daily for a fortnight, had far better effect : however, *perhaps*
the water, in the first instance, assisted to produce the renovation
I afterwards experienced.

XCVI.

Good claret is a liquor none need fear :
Champagne drinks ill from *small Madeira glasses* :
With such an host I'll seldom dine, I swear,
Who carefully his bottle slowly passes ;
I hate *attempts* at show, and empty vanity,*
Give me plain cheer, good breeding, and urbanity.

XCVII.

Good breeding's rather scarce, as is good news—
You meet them *sometimes* in Calcutta papers :
Where wit is wanting—anxious to amuse,
Green Editors will cut fantastic capers.
On other's labours journalists love feeding ;
'Mongst half a dozen—*two* may be worth reading.

---

* "*Vanity.*" I was once invited to dine with a gentleman at an
out station, almost a stranger to me. I felt obliged by his hospitality
—he *produced* Champagne for *show*, not drinking as *it appeared* : for
just as I was going to help myself to a bumper, in a moderate sized
claret glass after cheese, a servant seized on my glass, and on others,
placing *small Madeira* glasses in their stead. I looked at the servant, but in vain ; it was "*mine host's*" order, which of course prevented my tasting his *Simpkin*, as the natives call it.

XCVIII.

Oh, *Junius!* if thou livest, tell thy name,
And save the brains remaining of some driveller ;
How many million quires has thy fame,
To hunt thee out, foul *wasted* many a scribbler ?
They've turn'd and twisted *this* and *that* great man,
And ended just as wise as they began,

XCIX.

I hate to see an ass *act* like a mule,
Because a donkey is a patient creature ;.
Nor does it frisk, and flounder, scorning rule,
Its ears are long—and of more pensive feature.
Us'd to the road, from beaten tracks ne'er straying,
Without *some cause*, it seldom takes to *braying !*

* At one period, the Indian press was overwhelmed, stupified even
to *stultification*, with *writers, reasoners, argumentists, conjecturers,
schoolmasters, ushers, school-boys,* and *blockheads,* setting forth
who the *real Junius* was, or was *not :* but alas! Junius *still sleeps*
in *statu quo*—just as unknown as ever. Indeed, many a man in
England has tried his hand, on the same theme, but with *no proof,*
that can supersede conjecture.

C.

Mortals there are who think that Nature kind
(Where the cap fits, pray pardon the analogy ;)
Hath given them reason, wit, more strength of mind
Than some allow them—Critics in Phrenology :
Meek, modest youths, who fancy they were made
True Bards by nature, though poor *Subs** by *trade.*

CI.

'Tis certainly a failing with too many
To follow that, which nature ne'er ordained,
Or fitted them perchance for, least of any—
From which arose the awkward term " *hair-brained.*"
In some things men may shine, though not in others,
An useful hint to fathers, and to mothers.

* " *Subs by trade.*" Many is the young man (urged on by the
" *cacoethes scribendi*"—and the facility with which *some* Indian
editors of newspapers print all they can catch) who has been led to
commit the sin of " *prose run mad*" in the Calcutta journals—neglecting more profitable pursuits, to the loss of his own time, and
injury of his employers. How much better would such time have
been employed in the study of his professional duties? j

CII.

No boy should be foredoom'd to a profession,
Be it the army, church, sea, special pleading,
Or any other (pardon the digression),
Unless his genius be thereunto leading :
Or if he be, I venture to foretell,
'Gainst inclination,* he will ne'er excel.

CIII.

I'm no Phrenologist—nor do I care
Upon what peg they choose to hang these matters on ;
Yet, I have heard fair ladies who declare
They all believ'd the doctrinals of P——son.†

---

* "'Gainst inclination." Many a youth has been lost, by his
parents obliging him to follow a profession for which he had an
aversion, or disinclination ; and for which his genius never intended him. I have known young men in India, in the army, who de-
tested their profession, and cursed the day they ever quitted home
for India : one, in particular, had a most serious idea of resigning
his commission, were he but sure of obtaining the situation of a
stage coachman on his return to Europe.—Thus, how many parents
sacrifice their children with the idea, that a Cadetship to India
is a provision—the youth being forced on a profession he abhors,
and to a climate, where, in a short period, Death probably puts a
termination to his pining miserable existence.

† " P——t——son." This gentleman, who is in the medical line,
favoured the Calcutta public with lectures on Phrenology. He

Since most had found, and never had *they* gibed,
The *very bumps* our Doctor has described.

CIV.

'Tis all the fashion now, and more's the pity,
That people judge each other by their bumps ;
If *Doctor Spursheim* visited our city,
Some *clever fellow* might be in the dumps—
To find the brains which God had given, though small,
Had no one symptom in a *bump* at all !—

CV.

Folks now-a-days survey each others' skull,
And editors have different modes of feeling ;
Where nature forms our bumps too soft, or dull,
Blame not the owner, if you love plain-dealing :
If " *John Bull*" dies 'midst editorial fury
Let the " *Hurkaru*" face an " half-cast jury."*

had many disciples, both male and female ; still the majority of the
public were disposed to treat the theory with just ridicule.

* "*Hurkaru* and *John Bull*." The names of two Calcutta
newspapers, decided rivals and opponents. Great feuds in 1825
arose between them—each had its partizans—but in point of ability the *Hurkaru* stood pre-eminent. The utter annihilation of
Bull was thought to be approaching! The allusion to the *Hurkaru*

CVI.

Wit has its limits—this I merely hint—
'Tis very well when quarrels are not hatching :
We've all our troubles—curse on puny print,
And lean musquittoes, when they bite to scratching.
Yes, one among this city's minor evils,
Is blundering, stupid, half-cast *"printers' devils!"* *

CVII.

Careless compositors—type all astray—
Thin paper running into awkward spelling—
Half words—bad English—ev'ning dark or grey,
Much news—dim print—and patience not worth telling.
Close drizzling weather—joyous bull frogs greet us,
Answer'd by flying bugs, and starv'd musquittoes!

CVIII.

Yes, I have felt them, and have smelt them too :
At *flying bugs*† an English ear with wonder ;

being tried by a *half-cast* jury, is in reference to its editor having
strongly urged the propriety of that class being employed on *all*
juries as well as Europeans.

　* *"Printers' devils."* The *Calcutta* printers' devils sometimes
make astonishing *havoc* with common words, and common sense.

　† *"Flying bugs."* Towards the close of the rainy season swarms

Close was dull eve—earth steaming heat like dew,
Whilst distant echoes far resounded thunder—
Buzzing they came, in hungry desperation—
Soon, all was *scratching, stamping, puffing, perspiration.*

CIX.

Oh ye, on whom dame Fortune's favours smile,
Whose luck is seated near some snowy mountain—
Free from this sick'ning hemisphere of bile—
Cool spring your drink—no drug from soda fountain.
His fate I envy—keen for " *Cock a leecky,*"
And yearly visits *cheap,* to " *gude auld Reeky !*"

of these annoying insects, of a brown colour, resembling in shape small beetles with wings and scales, and emitting a very offensive smell, fly about towards night-fall, in all directions. I have witnessed them in such shoals in glass shades which enclosed the candles, as to have my eyes affected for two or three days after, from the force of their strong pungent effluvia. The musquittoes also are very large in the lower parts of Bengal, and bite very keenly at certain periods of the year, especially where the country is low and swampy. The above two stanzas contain an exact description of a September's evening, as many a resident in India has experienced.

* " *Gude auld Reeky.*" An ancient Scottish name for " Edinburgh Toon," known to most people—as is, I believe, the gude Scot's dish o' " *cock a leecky.*"

F

CX.

'Tis not the search of gain that yields contentment,
'Tis not far wand'ring o'er a distant land—
'Tis not war, glory, gratified resentment,
Nor victory, can happiness command.
Fortune may have a good or evil bent;
But he who roams, was *never* yet *content!*

CXI.

Stranger, whoe'er thou art, avoid all broils—
I don't mean *grills*, for here there's nought but *grilling*;
If thou'rt a soldier, bargain for turmoils—
In camp or quarters—guards, parades, and drilling.
Traders,—civilians,—venerate the laws,
And shun the touch of *Tipstaves'* greasy paws.

CXII.

I don't hate *lawyers*, still I think the world
Might very well afford to do without them :
A solemn air, black gown, and wig well curl'd,
Have doubtless fascinations strong about them.
Wisdom sits easy—but they all agree
To be blind, deaf, and *dumb*, without a *fee !*

CXIII.

" Law has no bottom"—this I've cause to know—
A good cause too, if heard to a conclusion :
Oh, were but British justice sure, as slow,
Then right and wrong might cease to cause confusion.
Law and its quibbles border on romancery,
The *worst of chances*, is a *" suit in Chancery !"**

CXIV.

Our Indian courts maintain contention strong—
We've *Wildes* and *Scarletts* here, in native pleaders ;
Their tongues, or purses, are not quite so long—
Plump Musselmans, I think, are chiefly leaders.
The fortune's made of any glib *Ramjohnny*,
Who fills a post in *" Sudder Court Dewanny !"*†

* *" Suit in Chancery."* The author for the last eight years has unfortunately been saddled with a *" suit in Chancery,"* which he is sorry to say appears to be as far distant from coming to a conclusion, as the first day on which it commenced—he therefore speaks *feel-ingly.*

† *" Sudder Court Dewanny."* This is the highest civil Court of the East India Company, and one of appeal, from the District Courts. *Ramjohnny*, or *Ramzanny*, is one of the most common names among the Musselmans of Bengal and Hindoostan. It some-times is used as a term of contempt by Europeans, and as a general

CXV.

This "Sudder Court" is one of high appeal—
Like Chancery—'tis seldom in a hurry—
Those who get in, oft glad are out to steal
With pockets taper—(Law's a dog will worry).
Keen Zemcendars* I've known with anger frothing,
Who would have *law*—they had it—not for *nothing !*

CXVI.

A " *Petty Court*"† may sometimes prove a pest,
Perhaps I'm treading upon ground that's tender :

name to their menials of the Musselman tribe, though the appellation, of course, when indiscriminately used, is incorrect, and perhaps offensive.

* "*Zemcendars.*" These are the landholders of the country, and meet consideration according to the property they possess. The land tax throughout Bengal was fixed by the late Marquis Cornwallis, and at a *very moderate* rate—but the exactions of Zemcendars from their tenants, are sometimes *exorbitant.*

† "*Petty Court.*" There is a Petty Court for the recovery of small debts, and for minor offences, held daily in Calcutta, where one of the magistrates presides. *Some* persons complain of the irregularities therein, with what justice I know not : but of this I am certain, that if such courts be efficiently conducted, they must prove of the *greatest benefit to the community.*

Of any evil, one should make the best—
Here, claims are heard 'gainst Master, Servant, Vender.
Commissioners attend—and sometimes saw
A knotty knob off some stale quirk of law.

CXVII.

I've done with Law—would it have done with me!
About *its blessings* I am quite decided :
Who knows it least—the happiest is he—
The nearest kin its power has divided.
There's Billy B——n* (if he be living still)
Can plan an heir, or help to make a will !

CXVIII.

The *will of man* is sometimes prone to error,
So laws were made to keep him fair and straight ;
But when relax'd, they lose all force and terror,
And then a Judge's voice is idle prate.
Had Death spar'd *Justice Elliot*,† many a thief
Would ne'er have touch'd his neighbour's bread or beef.

* " *Billy B—n.*" Hereby " *hangs a tail.*" Suffice it to say,
he was a Methodist—and tried his hand sometimes at a will.

† " *Justice Elliot.*" This gentleman was the *ne plus ultra* of
magistrates—the terror of thieves—the discoverer, the taker, and

CXIX.

Death sometimes proves a friend—sometimes a foe—
I say it, though on this Divines may differ—
And here thy scythe, grim Death, hath dealt a blow,
That if it would, it could not deal a stiffer
To this, our city—nor should it be forgotten
What *Elliot* did, though now his bones lie rotten.

CXX.

The pride of ancestry—the arm of power—
May raise a name, which else had been a blank ;
But give me *him*, whose acts will spring and flower
For public good—be high or low his rank—

punisher of *Dakoits*, and murderers. His death was deemed a
public loss, and afterwards proved (as I have been told) a public ca-
lamity to Calcutta, and its vicinity. I knew not the man, nor ever
saw him, but his indefatigability as a magistrate was *proverbial*—
his very *name* was sufficient to disperse whole gangs of the most
abandoned villains—for he spared no labour to discover their
haunts, and to make the most salutary examples. A *Dakoit* is a
highway robber, who ranges the country by land, or by water,
plundering and murdering—they sometimes go in gangs of 20 or
30 : but *Justice Elliot* hung up many a one for crows to feed
on, and thereby cleared lower Bengal of many a murderous villain.
" *Peace to his ashes*"—Calcutta may bewail him.

Let men like this (whatever be their station)
Meet due reward, with *public approbation!*

CXXI.

"Rome was not built in one day"—so's the saying;
Nor any other city that I know of—
Improvements now in ours are sore delaying,
Although of brick and mortar there's a show of.
Our native builders know the art of creeping,
And this fam'd Burmese war* has set all sleeping.

CXXII.

Calcutta, of its palaces high vaunting,
Shews not in grandeur equal to my wish—
A proper market very much is wanting:
What though *Tiretta's* boasts flesh, fowl and fish?
So throng'd—so dirty—one can scarce shove through it,
Upon my word 'tis a disgrace to view it.

* This was about the conclusion of the Burmese war, but public improvements were at a stand—plenty of Bank notes, and yet a wonderful scarcity of *hard cash,* in Calcutta. Plenty of bricks—mounds of mortar—but little doing. In truth, improvement on the City of Palaces, was at this time at a *nonplus.*

CXXIII.

Like to a ship, coop'd up 'mongst dirty sailors,
No room to walk—ropes, sails, or casks, on deck—
Hot sun above—thin creaking boards our jailors,
There's rub for rub—a white shirt with a check—
So in Tiretta—though free from tar and cables,
You're penn'd by *fish, fruit, flesh,* and *vegetables !**

CXXIV.

The simile, perhaps, you'll think far fetch'd—
I grant from boyhood I've been fam'd for skipping
Hop, step and jump—the thought may be far stretch'd
From mutton chops, to tatter'd sails and shipping.
Markets I've seen, and market-houses fine,
But, *Liverpool,* ne'er one to *equal thine !*

---

* *"Vegetables."* It is true, that *"Tiretta's Bazar"* contains all these, but so huddled together, that it is often disgusting to view them, covered by flies, and in a hot sun. Besides the above, there are fowls, rabbits, eggs, &c. &c. so that purchasers can scarcely squeeze through. One of the greatest improvements to Calcutta would be a large roomy market under proper regulation—with distinct divisions for fish, fruit, flesh, fowl, &c.

CXXV.

I've rambled a good deal by steam, and coaches,
By ships, and trackshuyts, for I hate to walk—
Upon one's purse, to see the world, encroaches;
But then, on what you've seen, you safe may talk.
Of all the sweet retirements worth a telling,
Calcutta " *Garden-houses*"* are excelling.

CXXVI.

The *Paunseway* on the Hooghly rapid rowing—
The pinnace gliding o'er its silver stream,
The stately ship, yards brac'd, with all sail flowing,
Gay flags, clear sky, soft music, like a dream—
The spicy breeze—grand balconies—neat planting—
To one from sea, seems Fairy-land enchanting.

* " *Garden-houses.*" So called in India, and country-seats in England. There is a curve in the river about four miles below Calcutta, called " *Garden reach.*" Here are beautiful country-seats, from which is a fine view of the *Hooghly*, with ships and boats of all kinds passing to and fro daily. These retirements are most grateful in March, April, May, and June, from the excessive heat and dust of Calcutta.

CXXVII.

But then, Sol's beams are felt—musquittoes bite—
In Autumn's eve, flies, bugs, infest your dwelling;
Huge croaking bull frogs hail the coming night,
Black buzzing beetles join shrill jackals' yelling—
The *spell's dis-pell'd*—and soon we wish to flee—
For ENGLAND dear—*what land can equal thee?*

CXXVIII.

Travel than books will reason more expand,
And smooth the zeal of bigots down to hearing—
What the eye views, the head may understand,
And liberality obtain a hearing.
Seclusion is a test the heart oft narrows on,
To judge correctly, all lies in *comparison.*

CXXIX.

The hour is come, when say I must ADIEU !
Farewell Calcutta, may kind Fate befriend ye—
I've strove to sketch your portrait in *one* view,
But leave to others, what some think might mend ye.
Bazars call'd *China, Burrah, Loll,* and *Jawn,*
With *other matters* I'll not touch upon.

CXXX.

Enough ! and here, my humble lay must end,
More might be said on Eastern modes, and fashions—
Split be the pen that aims to hurt a friend,
Or minister to base and sordid passions.
If for an hour my reader's care relaxes,
I'll bear with *physic, war, love, law and taxes !*

———o———

PASSING HINTS.

DEDICATED TO CERTAIN CALCUTTA LUMINARIES.

———o———

"Laugh then at any, but at fools or foes,
"These you but anger, and you mend not those—
"Laugh at your friends, and if your friends are sore,
"So much the better—you may laugh the more!"

POPE.

———o———

I LIKE Calcutta, when it's not too hot—
I like a good and comfortable table—
I like *fresh Loll—** of *Hodgson,*† too, a pot—
A pair of " *Bays,*" a curricle, a stable—
But as for " *Duns*" I leave *them* to posterity—
Curse on the name ! but pardon my asperity.

I like a play—provided not too long—
A rout, yclep'd a " *converzatione*"—

* An Indian word for *claret,* which I picked up in less than five
minutes, during my study of "*gastronomy*" at a friend's house.
Loll, however, literally signifies red.

† " *Hodgson.*" Fine ale, so called from the famed brewer's name.

Where comely dames with sense together throng,
Nor yet too plump, or manfully too bony ;
I like the sex, with mirth and graceful ease,
If not too free, with some kind *wish to please.*

I like an auction, when it's not too full—
Not W——re's though, when fill'd with rotten *cases* :
Tulloh's will do—there things are seldom dull,
Nor does it swarm with *demi-dingy* faces.
There you're " *knock'd down,*" with genuine agility,
And justice bids me add, with *much civility.*

I like a masquerade, when there's a ball :
A supper, too, good harmony advances—
Champagne, if *cool,* may whiz in the Town-hall—
There Quadrilles *do*—but not your *Kitchen dances :*
To foot an Irish jig, or Highland reel,
No lady *now* would be so - - - - - - *ungenteel !*

* What will some of our tip-top Calcutta ladies say, when they hear that the *finale* to a fashionable Countess, or Marchioness's ball in England, has been " Sir Roger de Coverly," or a *downright jig!* " O tempora ! O mores !"

I like *some* private parties—and *some not ;*
I like an hostess affable and civil—
Oh, could good breeding, like fine clothes, be bought,
Then one might obviate a passing evil—
Statues are very well in proper places,
But *ease* is an attribute of the Graces !*

I read two papers daily—sometimes four—
A friend to " *John,*"† " *Hurkaru,*" and the *News ;*
But it is trifling, Sir, and I feel sore,
That these two bucks should rob me of my dues.
Bid them renounce all puerile hostility,
Nor waste a column daily in scurrility.

I like good news—whene'er it chance to come,
The *Government Gazette* gives vile thin paper.
With you too, " *Indy,*"‡ I'm not quite at home,
Spare type doth ill agree with ev'ning taper—

---

* I have seen *some* ladies *stick* themselves up in their houses in
Calcutta to receive company, like *statues* to be worshipped—eheu!

† The Calcutta " *John Bull* " and the " *Hurkaru* " were at
this time at open war.

‡ " *Indy.* " The *India Gazette,* so called for shortness—the
best Journal, in 1825, in Calcutta.

And since in print I see you're sometimes tripping,
I vote your "Printer's Devils" *all a whipping!*

News *now* from Rangoon's like an April shower—
To read the "*Scotsman*"* I have no great *itch;*
A *Thistle* some maintain's a garden flower,
Yet still I think 'tis better in a *ditch*—
The Sunday papers, too, I seldom see,
I care as much *for them,* as they *for me!*

Th're those who're fond of *puppies*—let that be—
And others relish cats, tom-tits, and rabbits—
'Tis happy *all* our tastes do not agree,
Else mankind would not differ in their habits.
Some folks are easy pleased—(a goodly omen,)
Plain men I've often lik'd—but *not plain women.*

I've told you what I like, but I like more
Whom I'll not notice here—though still I might;
For they are "*far away*" on Britain's shore—
Oh! "*far away*"—and I must bid good night.
So if you'll please to pardon my sincerity,
I'll tell you what *I hate* with more dexterity.

* "*Scotsman.*" This paper shortly after died a natural death.

THE MUSICIANS.

A TALE.

"Let Care's dull sons with gloomy malice rail,
"May mirth be still the hero of our tale."

Come, Mistress Muse, since you scout prose,
At humble verse don't cock your nose;
Ah! smiling come—no sharp retort—
Don't say the story's stale and old,
A good thing, sure, may be twice told,
Especially when sweet and short.
One word is left—so don't feel sore,
This tale was ne'er in rhyme before;
Besides, Ma'am, I would have you know
'Tis no first cousin to *old Joe !**
A funny fellow, whose relations
Are well received by divers nations;

---

* Few are the people who have not heard of, or read the jokes
of that funny wight, *Joe Miller.*

G

Right welcome guests—though in the East
They seldom grace a Hindoo's feast.
Mouths, as *they* say, are made to eat,
So Hindoos think a joke's a cheat,
Invented merely to give trouble,
To interrupt the *Hubble Bubble ;*
Did old Joe's self begin to spout,
A whole *Punchuet*† would kick him out—
Though one, and all, delight to *smoke,*
They never scratch to find a joke ;
Unless said joke may end in toddy,
Or rubbing oil upon the body ;
Stale, far-fetch'd thoughts upon the price
Of *Cowries‡—Dhal—Milk—Ghee,* and rice.
On these—inspir'd with *Toddy's* glow,
They sometimes draw a swinging bow ;
If servants, they will talk the faster,
And scan the good and ill of Master.

---

* A name not uncommon for an Hindoostanee pipe, and very expressive of the nature and sound of that muddling instrument.

† An assemblage of people of the same cast in India, who meet to discuss and to determine any point of difference arising among each other. They also assemble to celebrate marriages, and the like.

‡ " *Cowries,*" small shells, the lowest denomination of Bengal currency.—*Dhal,* split peas—*Ghee,* clarified butter.

How cautious is each honest soul,
To say how much his neighbour stole;
On this they all know—old and young—
" A wise head keeps a silent tongue."
Free-mason like—you'll find no croaker,
To tell about a spit, or poker;
No—all the little imps in H—ll
May singe them *white,* before they'll tell.
Yet should, perchance, one drunken brother,
Expose the misdeeds of another,
The wicked, blundering, tell-tale sinner,
Must patch his cast, and give a dinner;
For here, the sin lies not in stealing,
But on the circumstance revealing.

   First, invitations fly around,
Next *Hubble Bubbles* quick resound—
Like sober Aldermen they sit,
Who blink at Waithman's city wit—
Wonder, and stare, but nothing drop—
Unless the number of their shop.
Just so our Hindoos—men of sense,
Feast seldom at their own expense;
With them, no entertainment's dull
Provided there's a *belly-full;*

Cross-legg'd they squat—but seldom chatter—
Unless *Caste, Pice, Grain, Ghee's* the matter ;
And then 'tis vain to know what's said,
They'd talk old mother K——n dead.

But whither, Madam, do you ramble,
Is this a subject for preamble ?
To treat about the poor Hindoos,
You might as well attack the Jews ;
Or vent your spleen on Whig and Tory—
Pray what have Hindoos with the story ?
Commence your tale in humble lays,
As Authors all do now-a-days ;
And to the world freely give
An honest, simple narrative ;
Without evasion or disguise,
Like modern writers—write *no lies.*

" *Once on a time,*"—aye, " *that's your sort*"—
Two frisky fellows, fond of sport,
Who seldom thought on where, or when ;
Despis'd mean cringing to the great,
Laugh'd at dull coxcombs aping state,
Both, Pay and Batta gentlemen :*

* Officers of the army. Alluding to a Calcutta lady, who, on
being asked her opinion of a military gentleman for a husband,
made answer, " *None of your pay and batta gentlemen for me !*"

With purses that could bear a pull,

(Those were the days of " *double full*" *)

In an old *Budgerow*† came down,

To rummage all the shops in town.

Stepping ashore at *Chaudpaul-Ghaut*‡

You'd swear they were but newly caught;

For they had liv'd five years or more,

On mutton commons at Cawnpore;

And better mutton, too, I trow,

Than in *Calcutta's* market *now*.

'Tis true, they sometimes got by *Dawk*‖ up

Smok'd *mango-fish*,§ and rotten *cockup*—

So bad, yet so extremely dear,

They only had them once a year;

---

* " *Double full.*" This means " double full batta," an allowance made to all the troops in the field, and in the Vizier of Ande's dominions, but done away with by the Marquis of Wellesley's government. *Cawnpore* is a station on the river Ganges, above seven hundred miles from Calcutta.

† " *Budgerow.*" A round-bottomed boat, built for travelling on the river Ganges.

‡ " *Chaudpaul-Ghaut.*" This is a favourite landing-place in Calcutta.

‖ " *Dawk*" means Post.

§ *Cockup* and *mango-fish* are the two finest sea fish in Bengal— the latter are only procurable in April, May, and beginning of June.

And once a year was quite enough,

To pay for such confounded stuff.

But now arrived on cockup ground,

They'd have them fresh if to be found ;

So long in dull cantonment cloisters,

They'd quite forgot the shape of oysters !

Still worse, the laws and sacred rules

Of all the dancing boarding-schools.*

" 'Twas passing strange"—they scarce knew how

To flirt a fan—to smirk, or bow ;

To lecture o'er a masquerade,

Or scan how gowns and caps were made,

Though both could open *on parade.*

What weighty bus'ness had this pair

(You'll ask) to breathe Calcutta air ?

Arrange your *spec.'s,* Sir, rub them clean—

Fun, dancing, cockup, change of scene !

Though here one may as well confess,

They'd been commission'd—by a mess

---

* " *Dancing boarding-schools.*" At the most fashionable ladies'
seminaries in Calcutta, there were dances given two days in the
week, to which young gentlemen were admitted, and there they
sometimes fell in love, and became *Benedicts.* This practice, I believe, still prevails in *some* schools, though at one time it fell into
disrepute.

Of jolly dogs, who lov'd good cheer,
To buy up claret, cheese and beer;
And for their very lives and souls,
Not to forget *two* huge punch bowls:
In case their memories might slip,
'Twas " *Mem: to hold eight quarts of flip.*"
The last was broke one afternoon,
When keeping up the *fourth of June;*
In a fam'd raffle, some one won it,
'T had Toby Philpot's face upon it,
With carbuncles as big as sloes,
Fix'd on a rubicond huge nose.
As cash and credit might run low,
They brought a draft on Trail and Co.
Since here they were resolv'd to stay
To make the most of night and day,
Whilst aught remain'd to pay the way.

In half a house, near Larkin's Lane,
This pretty pair had lodgings ta'en;
The other half a Frenchman claim'd—
Blest with no children, and no wife,
A year he'd dwelt there free from strife,
Of two such lodgers never dream'd.

As most of Frenchmen like to chat,
He kept a parrot, and a cat;
Besides a handy servant Boy,
Jaques was his name—his master's joy:
Who fed poor Puss—took care of Poll—
And serv'd as butler, cook, and all!
A famous fellow was this Jaques,
For cooking Currys, Grills, and steaks;
But set him to—to roast or boil,
Monsieur oft swore, " *Got tam you spoil!*"
Our Frenchman, once of good condition,
Rather than starve, had turn'd Musician:
In hopes (like other refugees)
To *scrape* a fortune by degrees.
His custom, though not grand, was *good*,
It found him lodging, clothes, and food.
What more could any man desire,
'Twas *hot enough* without a fire;
And as Calcutta boasted few,
One house in those days serv'd for two.
　Now, Mistress Fate ordain'd it so
They liv'd above—Monsieur below—
But as the rooms above were small,
Stairs ill contriv'd for friends to call:

" *Plaguey unhandy*" to get up,
Should strangers stop to dine, or sup ;
The first thing these wights thought about,
Was, how to *roast* the Frenchman out !
Old is the maxim, and well known
That " Satan's kind unto his own"—
So, scarce to think had they began,
Before *Sir Nickey* laid the plan :
That arch inventor of all evil,
(Styl'd Buonaparte* by some) the Devil—
Made them resolve that very day,
To charm old Pan in his own way.
As Monsieur fill'd them with delight,
Teaching dull scholars, near and far,
By day, flute, fiddle, and guitar,
They swore they'd tune their pipes *by night !*
Two friends select, next ev'ning came,
Who mightily approv'd the scheme.
'Twas fair to sing, and where the crime
To beat a floor in treble time ?

Scarce Monsieur to his bed had crept,
(Just underneath he always slept)

* When this was written, Buonaparte was in the zenith of his
fame.

Disrob'd of bag, wig, cue, and clothes,
Tired and ready for a doze,
Than these campaigners, void of care,
Sung, danc'd, thump'd table, floor, and chair.
Lost in amazement and dismay,
The Frenchman, cat, and parrot, lay.
With face demure, and thought profound,
Five hours pass'd—he roll'd in bed,
Turn'd right—then left—now scratch'd his head,
Next look'd—then mutter'd at the sound—
" Is it de birth-day of deir King
" Dat vor make all dis chorus ring !
" No man at all, dans le grand nation
" Could chant so loyal an oration.
" Be gar, me do not like dis fun,
" I vis dem Englisman vere gone ;
" Oh ! such Diable contre danse,
" Mine Got ! me neber see in France !"
    Alas ! poor Monsieur little thought
He two such Tartar youths had caught—
'Twas some grand gala they did keep ;
Like other folks they might regale,
Once in a way with songs and ale,
Next night he'd have his dose of sleep :

Recover what he'd last foregone,
And snooze from dusk till morning's dawn.
　　Day soon roll'd on—oh! fie for shame,
Next ev'ning brought the self-same game—
A piteous game—more loud and hoarse,
If one may judge of night's annoy
By a harsh fiddle, and hautboy—
A rolling drum now lent its force !
On this they made most furious rattle,
Worse than the " *Pas de charge*" in battle ;
Their fav'rite air—a charming song,
With winding chorus loud and long,
(Enough to make a Frenchman sore)
Was " *Rule Britannia*,"—with *encore !*

　　In sleepy rage, and sullen gloom,
Monsieur stalk'd up and down the room—
No human form could have slept,
Feet, drum, voice, fists, sweet chorus kept—
The hour of night just half-past ten,
Awhile he sat, then pac'd again—
Now bit his nails—next stamp'd the floor—
Look'd fierce—first op'd, then shut the door—
With visage pale and wig awry—
At last he spoke—first heav'd a sigh :

" Mine Got ! mine Got ! dis be too bad,

" De Englismans ave all runn'd mad;

" Jaques, go and tell (mine lad, be cleber)

" De gentlemans, I've got de feber—

" Poor master seick and very ill,

" To-night he take de *leetel peill !* "

    Away went Jaques, with piteous face,

To tell his lamentable case;

But where the use in Jaques to go ?

" Because an English jubilee

" Must (as they said) with jocund glee,

" Be kept until the cock should crow—

" The night before, he sure had warning,

" They'd sung him " *Lango Lee*" till morning;

" And as the music, fun, and freaks,

" Would only last about three weeks,

" They could not stop when just begun,

" For any living mother's son.

" No ! if his grand-dad from the grave

" Should rise, they'd tip him t'other stave."

Poor Jaques's face did strongly presage,

The sad result of Monsieur's message;

Who scarcely knowing how to look,

Strove (but in vain) to hum *Malbrook,*

Imploring first to grant him aid
One of those heathen heavenly elves,
(Who help us when we can't ourselves)
Styl'd sweet *Miss Patience*, meek-ey'd maid.
She came, and in a cruel stew
Found Monsieur thinking what to do,
Who shrugg'd his shoulders with a grin,
" Tree weeks de keep dis hellish din !
" O'tres bien—me soon vil see
" If de sing up veeks von, two, tree ;
" De Franceman he good vatch can keep—
" De Englisman first eat, den sleep !"
  Be this, however, as it may,
Our rogues had turn'd night to day ;
Whilst Monsieur and his scholars scrap'd,
These pretty youths fast snoring gap'd—
And thus refresh'd with force amain,
Were ready for a fresh campaign.

  Four waking nights our Frenchman pass'd,
Hoping each night might prove the last ;
Sometimes a sigh and oft a groan,
To soften each discordant tone ;
For Ma'amselle Patience being loth
To hear us mortals swear an oath,

Plain told Monsieur 'twere all in vain
To take God's name in angry strain:
In furious rage to rant and curse,
Would only make the matter worse;
Better to grin, mild calmly bearing,
They'd not leave off for all his swearing.
A goodly lesson this she taught,
If men would practise what they ought,
But Patience' voice (like dogg'rel rhymes)
Can only please at certain times—
Resign'd and calm her empire sways,
Till Passion darts her venom'd rays—
Seizes the heart—misleads the mind—
And rules distracted human kind.

  Just so, alas! on the fifth night,
Poor mild *Miss Patience* took her flight—
When lo! came bouncing in her place
(No wonder Monsieur scarce could blink,
Four nights he had not slept a wink)
*Megæra** with her frightful face!
Such harsh, discordant, deep-ton'd music
Was fit to set a whole ship's crew sick;

  * One of the Furies—Goddess of rage and anger.

Had they stuck to an English glee,
One might have borne the minstrelsy;
But as for mischief they grew riper,
They'd hir'd an Hindoostanee piper—
A fellow who could blow in style
A trump, that sounded half a mile;
With such variety of sounds,
Worse than a mongrel pack of hounds,
You'd thought Hell's imps had grown disloyal,
And fought Old Nick a battle-royal:
Though Sleep's dull god had done his best,
'Twere vain—no mortal could find rest;
For such a noise, and dismal roar,
The neighbours never heard before.

Monsieur scarce sunk in Morpheus' arms,
Free as he thought from war's alarms,
Quick started from his sleep in fear,
Whilst *row dow dow* assail'd his ear:
When, more his senses to confound,
Harsh came the trumpet's squeaking sound,
With dismal and discordant scream—
Our Frenchman thought 'twas all a dream,
Felt right and left, and where the ground,
First rubb'd his eyes—then star'd around—

Next for poor Jaques aloud did call,
Then strove to drown the trumpet's squall.
"Pardonnez moi—A! sacre Dieu,
"Monsieur! Messieurs! que voulez vous?
"*Ah! misericorde*—vat's dis I hear,
"Again it sounds upon mine ear—
"*Oh, morbleu! peste! le ventre bleu!*
"'Tis vorse—Diable!—tam Hindu!
"Jaques, vere is Jaques?—Jaques! come, mine lad,
"*Le cri horrible*—set me mad."

Obedient Jaques (in better plight,
Got sleep by day, though none by night)
With gaping mouth, and folded hands,
Before his master silent stands,
Ready to swallow sage commands.
Fierce as our Frenchman curs'd and swore,
The drum and trumpet play'd the more—
At ev'ry oath, or furious scold,
The trumpet sounded—drum it roll'd—
E'en humble Jaques was vex'd at heart,
To see his sleepy master's smart—
To find that neither threats nor prayers,
Could stop the concert above stairs.

Whilst pacing up and down the room,
Fled had the Frenchman's fiery fume,
For passion, like a stormy sea,
Rages and foams, then dies away—
So in this instance stood the rule,
Megæra bows to *Prudence* cool—
Reason and *Patience* in her train,
And Monsieur is himself again.

Now consultation they pursue,
And judge of what is best to do;
For Jaques, in weightiest affairs,
Was burthen'd with his master's cares :
In conduct dutiful—yet free,
An honest, faithful soul was he.
When knotty points one comes upon,
"Two heads are better far than one."
Jaques spoke his mind, as servants should
When trusted for their master's good ;
The best of law was (by his creed)
To poor folks but a broken reed—
Great men of fortune it might fit,
But for poor souls an endless pit.
How many by the cautious laws
Are ruin'd, though they gain their cause !

H

How many live in vain to curse,
A foul defendant's length of purse—
Law will attend a great man's gate,
Whilst on the law the poor must wait.
Thus reason'd Jaques, who well did know
His Master's purse was plaguy low;
Who though he felt revengeful sore,
Still conn'd the matter calmly o'er;
At sound of law look'd wondrous big—
Yet doubtful paus'd, and teaz'd his wig;
In various light the matter sees,
But worst of all *Attorney's fees!*
Nor need the sages here be told,
That law is bought, and dearly sold—
In India, as in other climes,
It moves alert to golden chimes;
For nothing clears a lawyer's brains,
More than the chink of *gold's* pure strains.
The question now to issue came
(Quiet and Prudence versus Shame—)
Whether to stay, or quickly go,
Reason said *Move*—but Pride said *No*—
For though Monsieur had much approv'd
His servant's hints—still spirit mov'd.

At length meek Jaques's voice prevails,
And drowsy Morpheus sinks the scales—
Again the drum and trumpet play—
Resolv'd it was, *to move next day*.

Scarce had gay Phœbus ting'd with red
The curtains on our Frenchman's bed,
Than man and master sleepless sad,
Began to pack what goods they had;
For few the chattels, be it known,
That Monsieur well could call his own.
A blunderbuss without a lock—
A tarnish'd mirror—wig, and block—
Four aged chairs—a viol bass—
A liquor case, with lock of brass:
Old fashion'd plates, and glasses few,
Two pans for fricassee, or stew;
A table—fiddle—and guitar—
The former cut with many a scar,
The latter open, prone to jar:
A cuckoo clock, that once did chime—
With other traps scarce worth a rhyme.
Monsieur, however, made a blaze
At concerts, and on holidays—

A coat now grey, that once was green;
With lace that had much service seen :
Huge metal buttons Flanders milt,*
Of tinge to prove they had been gilt ;
A velvet waistcoat, reddish hue,
Trimmings of silver, turn'd to blue :
Nor need description modest blush,
Grey were his hose—his breeches plush :
In days of yore so good a pair,
Might serve to decorate *Rag Fair* :
A rotten trunk contain'd his gear,
The best, a little worse for wear:
Still more his wardrobe to enhance,
A pair of jack boots brown as dust,
A small sword half devour'd by dust,
A *chapeau*, " a-la-mode de France :"
And last, not least, to sum up all,
Came *Jaques*, *Grimalkin*, and *poor Poll !*

At usual hour the scholars come
Hoarse fiddle and guitar to thrum.
Our Frenchman's visage sad did low'r,
They found him busy, vex'd, and sour.

* This word is not common, and signifies coin milled, or struck.
Vide, Johnson.

The cause inquire—" What sudden notion

" Had urg'd this unexpected motion ?

" If aught had happen'd in the night,

" To cause-alarm, or speedy flight ?"

Since some suspected, what they saw

Was hasten'd by the force of law.

In piteous voice—dispos'd to cry,

Poor Monsieur answer'd—" *Raison vy !*

" Vell you may say—vy move de shair,

" Be Gar, de cause I tell you sair,

" Himself—Diable ! be up de stair.

" Five night he keep le cris pell mell,

" Dat trompe—œuf ! make horrible yell ;

" 'Tis vorse, mine Got ! dan imp of bell.

" Dis, and no autre is de raison,

" Vy I go seek une autre maison !"

Resolv'd no longer there he'd dwell,

Nor bear another five nights' spell,

That very day our Frenchman hired

Just such a house as was required.

Cool he departs, whilst gladsome they

(To cheer old Pan upon his way)

Resound the trump for *victory !*

Yet let it still be understood,
Though wild in thought, their hearts were good ;
To shew 'twas only fun they meant,
(And gain the house their sole intent)
They paid arrears of six months' rent.
Appearances, though sometimes strong,
Are not unfrequent in the wrong ;
So with this trait the story ends—
Though Monsieur's wroth at first arose
Against these youths, as bitter foes,
They prov'd *at last his best of friends :*
Freed him from duns, when wanting bail,
And *all the horrors of a jail!*

THE HIGHLANDER.

A TALE.

———0———

"Homines amplius oculis quam auribus credunt."

SENECA.

Men always will (the maxim's just)
Place more in eyes, than ears, their trust.

———0———

A HIGHLANDER, in former days,
In search of " means" as well as " ways,"
To Edinborough's* city came,
A town for *roses* mark'd by fame;
For lofty houses, grey with dirt,
From windows dangling smock, or shirt;
'Midst Highlands known for " Gowd, and leeks,"†
For Lairds " wi' stockins, brogues, and breeks."
  'Twas one hot summer's afternoon,
This Highland laddie " cam to Toon"—

* The old Town.
† The gardens around Edinburgh were famed for the finest leeks
(or onions) in Scotland—in days of yore.

Tir'd and dirty—fond of chat—
In the first ale-house down he sat;
Glad of the place his eye caught first
To rest his bones, and quench his thirst;
" Right fond o' *brie*,* he ken't nae fash,
" Owre gude auld halesom *Farintash*."†
But lest description prove a riddle,
The house was call'd the " *Cat and Fiddle :*"
Well known to soldiers, and to sailors,
To dustmen, tinkers, smiths, and tailors;
To all, whose *Patriotic* views
Led them to smoke, and read the news;
And vent their spleen in curses hearty,
On Talleyrand, and Buonaparté.

    After refreshment duly ta'en,
To see the *Toon* he was "*fu' fain.*"
Eager for sights, and raree-shows,
Dress'd in new bonnet—Sunday clothes—
So neat, so spruce, the lad appear'd
As if he'd been some Highland Laird.
Though shoes were new, and pinch'd him sore
(Since shoes he never wore before)

---

* " *Brie*"—strong drink. " *Nae fash*"—no harm.
† The finest and strongest whiskey in Scotland.

Yet loose or tight, 'twas all the same,
For gaily off he set, half lame ;
The weather calm, the moon shone bright ;
And by most clocks past ten at night.

  As on, with limping pace, he walk'd,
He to himself sagacious talk'd :
In wonder gaz'd, as he drew nigh
To houses seven stories high—
" The like were never to be seen
" At Inverness, or Aberdeen :
" In Isle o' Skye, or Sutherlan,
" Nae Laird could sic a hoose commaun;
" When hame I gang our Kate shall knaw
" Of a' the bonnie sights I saw—
" I'll owre the ingle mither tell,
" A' what I've view'd, and see'd mysel !"

  Thus much he to himself had said—
A window open'd over head—
Straight up he look'd, with Highland grin,
To spy what Goddess was within.
" War heeds ! war heeds !" he heard the call,
Then gap'd to see what goods might fall :
When, lo ! down pour'd what feeble words,
Or decency, no rhyme affords.

Splash falls a potent nauseous show'r,

Worse than Xantippe once did pour

(Enraged as the story says,)

O'er the bald pate of Socrates !

   Our Highlander ta'en unawares,

Began to cross,* and say his prayers ;

Yet, not before these words swift ran,

" Gude wife ! gude wife ! haud you haun ;

" Nae muckle De'il hae ye to fear,

" I only cam the way to spier ;

" At yon braw Kirk to tak a glint,

" Na thinkin ony hearm in't ;

" To see the Toon—ah ! sad my waes—

" Ye've splatter'd a' my Sunday claes !"

   Though glibly utter'd, evil fate

Ordain'd the sound should come too late.

The " gude wife," at the dismal call,

Popp'd out her head, and thus did squall :

" What near our hoose for do ye wait,

" Gad's curse, mun, can't ye gang your gait ?

" Your fearfu' skrieghs† maun a' affright,

" I wonna sleep a blink to-night.

  * Great numbers of the Highlanders are Roman Catholics.

  † " *Skrieghs*," shouts.

" Hech ! mon, don't skirl,* na mair keep grievin,

" I hae sma' doubts ye hae been thievin ;

" And gin ye dinna take your heels,

· " I'se gar ye rue your manfu' squeels :

" I'll ca' the watch (a' fast asleep)

" And gie ye to their muckle keep.

" Ye ken, what our gude Provost's will is

" Wi' sic as you, ye midnight billies ;

" Nae longer use to be a talkin,

" Sae scrieve, my codger, like a mawkin !"

   This said, our sorry Highlandman

Back to his lodgings limping ran ;

Lamenting o'er his hapless case,

Whilst putrid filth ran down his face :

His fine new clothes besmear'd and soil'd,

His bonnet, breeks, and jerkin spoil'd.

The Landlord nos'd him as he came

All dripping, vex'd with stench, and shame.

He told his tale—the best he could,

And easily 'twas understood.

" Nae longer in sic parts he'd stay,

" Just rest himsel anither day ;

* " Skirl," yell. " Billies," young rakes. " Scrieve," to run.
" Mawkin," a hare.

" *Roup** shoon, breeks, stockins, a', and then

" In kilts return straight hame agen.

" Hech ! what a trick to play on strangers !

" He'd rin nae mair this Toon's *foul dangers.*"

His host (but logic was in vain)

Advis'd the laddie to remain.

'Twas not at strangers p—ts were aim'd,

Nor was the " gude wife" to be blam'd ;

" *War heeds !*" was warning known to all,

To keep their distance from the wall :

To such, as in their dress were nice,

He'd venture with this sound advice—

Never to seek for shows or sights

In Edinburgh's " *auld Toon*" by nights ;

Since any sleepy, wicked woman,

Would "haud her haun a wee," for no man :

Prince, Lord, or Lady, friend, or foe,

Would fare the same were they below—

The wisest way to stay at home,

Nor after *sights* at midnight roam.

Lost was all talk—in doleful pet

Our Highlander straight homeward set ;

* Characteristic of a Highlander—that nothing should be lost.
" *Roup*" signifies an auction.

Reason prov'd vain, though the kind host,
With honest *Saunders* did his most.
Rather he'd toil 'midst hail, and sleet,
'Till blisters rose upon his feet;
Starve with his clan, steal, beg, or borrow,
Than trust himself in Edinborough!

A moral from this tale appends—
That ignorance to evil tends.
How many, time and judgment waste,
Who sport opinions form'd in haste;
Like this poor lad, who, 'midst his glen,
Swore p—ts were sav'd for Highlandmen;
And told the clan, who wistful listen'd,
How he himself had so been christen'd.
Thus, travellers o'er foreign climes
May blacken habits into crimes—
Custom misconstrue rude neglect—
Mere accident, to disrespect.
Men of true knowledge, wit, and sense,
Will ne'er seek cause to take offence;
But calm review things, states, and men,
And *understand, ere they condemn.*

SOBER HINTS.

DEDICATED TO AN INDIAN VOYAGE.

" Manners with fortunes, humours turn with climes,
"Tenets with books, and principles with times."

POPE.

I.

" ENGLAND, with all thy faults, I love thee still".*—
Just so said I, when last I quitted Dover,
And say again—return'd off Portland's Bill,
Thy chalky cliffs I view as would a lover
Expectant of sweet smiles, and greeting blisses,
Free, happy land of liberty, and kisses!

II.

'Twas with a sadden'd soul when last we parted,
Wind fresh, and free—and Falmouth dim to view—
The thought nigh sicken'd, as the tear slow started
For those, perhaps, I'd bid a last adieu.

* The above line is quoted from *Cowper*, and does him honour.

I felt *I dont know how*, at heart and gizzard,
When towards grey of eve we pass'd the *Lizard*.*

III.

Next morning came—but, Britain, thou wert gone !
We thought the Sun in rising rather lazy ;
Though up he'd got—but kept his night-cap on,
Which made the horizon look dim and hazy.
The wind blew keenly whistling through the shrouds,
But, *Albion*, in thy stead were waves and clouds.

IV.

Fond did we gaze—no land to bless the eye—
The distance bounded by the snowy billow,
As the ship roll'd—the heart stole forth a sigh,
And sore reflections hover'd near my pillow;
But " *Hope, sweet Hope*"—'twas thou, that eas'd the
            smarting,
So much for *thee*, and *England*—dear at parting.

V.

Those only know who leave their native land
For many a year, to stray in climates burning—

* The Lizard in Cornwall was the last land we saw of old England.

The feeling more than joy, to view the strand
Which distant hope held forth to their returning.
It is not health, love, comfort, joy, variety,
But all united, mix'd with strange anxiety.

VI.

What, some may ask, has this to do with *hinting* ?
If you'll go on, kind Sir, you'll find it may ;
The Muse will sometimes take a fit of squinting,
And leer, and ogle in a wanton way—
Just as the maggot bites, her subject varies,
Like flirting Misses, stung by strange vagaries.

VII.

Dear Madam, leave your freaks, and go on right—
Don't fancy other matters, or sit leering,
Pray recollect your promises last night,
At sober sense and metre, no more sneering—
'Tis lucky I'm not of a temper jealous,
Else *Hogg*, and *Southey** both, might " blow the bellows."

---

* Having a high respect and admiration for the poetic genius which distinguishes these great names, I hope they will pardon the mention of them, should accident ordain either of them hearing of this.

VIII.

Ha! here she flies—relief to latent woes,
Ship board her theme—and briefly shall we treat it—
Should hearers listen—Reader, blow your nose,
And in smooth accents gracefully repeat it.
Hard is *his* fate, whose Muse is left to spellers,
Damn'd both by critics, and enrag'd booksellers!

IX.

How few, fair *Albion*, of thy sons *not* glad
To see *thy shores*, and have a voyage ended!
A passage, be it middling, good, or bad,
Has many minor comforts fit to mend it.
Good breeding is a test, when long together,
It smooths down hot, cold, calm, or stormy weather.

X.

I never relish'd *cant* 'bout liberal feeling,
Though glad to see it with a liberal mind;
" *Works, and not words,*" are surest in plain dealing—
The one are solid, and the other wind.
No mark'd allusion's meant in what may follow,
I skim the surface, like a gull, or swallow.

I

XI.

This simile, perhaps, may poze the reader,
'Tis just as well the matter to explain—
You've seen a swallow skim (a hungry feeder)
Hunting pond flies—low, to and fro again—
Dipping its wings, but careful of a wetting—
Just so, take we all fish that strike our netting.

XII.

A ship is not a place to find much pity;
Where every person strives to help himself—
What's fun to sailors, landsmen don't deem witty,
Dancing, or fiddling, or a waste of pelf.
Most passengers like *air, light, books,* and *quiet,*
With little motion, and *good generous diet.*

XIII.

Where people meet train'd up in different ways,
With different morals, manners, ranks, and callings—
Led by their various tastes, as temper sways,
Gentle or rude, or fond of sottish brawlings—
Lively or lean, or dull from round obesity—
True wisdom here " *makes virtue of necessity.*"

XIV.

'Tis not agreeable when weather's cross,
Or the Commander of the vessel more so—
Enough, 'gainst wind obliged to tack and toss,
And face deep Ocean's angry waves that roar so:
To see a Captain dumb, and sullen looking,*
Spoils any dinner, howe'er good the cooking.

XV.

Calms, too, are trying subjects long at sea,
The source of spleen, ill breeding, and bad humour;
'Tis then, most fault is found with wine or tea—
Time seems to flag, and every air is rumour:
Of heaven's breath though not an air be stirring,
Ill natured stories " catching wind," go whirring.

XVI.

Of characters the worst to damn a ship,
Is a low-minded, prying, sly tale-bearer;
Where such is found, be guarded how you slip
A word, or joke—you'll hear it, though not fairer,

* I am sorry to observe it, but it is nevertheless too true, that Captains are frequently too much affected by the weather—some have been likened to walking thermometers.

Retail'd again, with wonderful immensity;
Most story-tellers lose nought by *condensity.*

XVII.

Such keep at distance, of their touch beware—
Reptiles, the scum, vile vipers of society.
Dancing and music soften time and care;
Cards, chess, backgammon, play'd with due sobriety,
Cheat tyrant Time—how many late bemoan him—
Faster he speeds, the longer one has known him.

XVIII.

Yes, *Time*, both ships and waves, thou far outstrippest,
The winds themselves have little chance with thee;
My good old fellow, glibly as thou trippest,
Just wait a while, and let a body *see!*
Upon one's *eyes* and *toes* why thus keep treading,
You're in a *cursed hurry* grey hairs spreading.

XIX.

I wish I'd known thee better somewhat sooner—
Good reader, if thou'rt doom'd to wear a wig,
'Tis probable *Time* sees thy afternoon, or
With some dear fair one wouldst thou " *run a rig?*"

A wig may hide grey hairs which *Time* besprinkles,—
But tell me, what can cure *dim eyes* and *wrinkles?*

XX.

Or gouty toes—when children work with chairs—
Oh cruel! from their reach one scarce can hobble,
To bed-room cold—up two long pair of stairs—
And then such pain, attended with such trouble.
I blame *thee, Time*—take breath—just let us pause,
Though doctors say fat turtle soup's the cause!

XXI.

Well, *Time*, upon the whole thou'rt worth respecting;
Last thirty years, on *some* I've seen thee shine—
Enjoy'd thee always, now and then excepting
A week on board a ship, when near the Line:
Then, wert thou dull, head-aching, and perspiring—
I'm sure *fat ladies* must have thought thee *tiring*.

XXII.

And lean ones, too—becalm'd, perhaps, for weeks—
Eager for thee, dear Britain—fresh stock thinner—
Sol in his zenith, dolphins cutting freaks;
But not one caught to help a meagre dinner—

Penn'd up with such, as common breeding scorning,
Stare in your face, nor deign to *nod good morning.*

XXIII.

Annoyances may spring from dogs, or cats,
Too early, or too long, thin boards a rubbing;
Cock-roaches eating books, clothes—mice, or rats;
And dirty leaks above, when decks are scrubbing:
*Stewing** is bad enough, there's no denying,
And last, not least, *spoilt petted children crying!*

XXIV.

Ah! many a melting moment, *Sol,* I've borne thee,
Glad of some shelter from thy sick'ning power;
But *now,* dear gentle youth, how oft I mourn thee,
Rejoic'd to see *thy phiz* peep through a shower.
Hail'd both by girls and boys, when hay is shaking—
You ne'er view'd aught, I hope, but fair hay-making!

XXV.

This is a profile of *thy visage, Time,*
And may have struck *some* traveller's perceptions,

* The Sun near the Line is sometimes *cruelly* hot, and then
shipmates grow tired of each other's company.

Who've seen good breeding scoff'd at as a crime ;
But partial whims have general exceptions.
A ship's not just the school to learn *gentility*,
Think yourself well, *if treated with civility.*

XXVI.

'Tis never pleasant to throw hints away,
Nor have fair wishes scorn'd, or unattended to—
To eat tough fowls, or mutton every day,
When, void of let or cost, such could be mended too,
Is rather grating, and I can't help saying,
Shews want of feeling, after *liberal paying.* *

XXVII.

Such traits as these cause stiffness, gloom, disgust,
Far more than mice, ants, cock-roaches, or leakings ;
A rough demeanour ever breeds distrust
Of what may follow—like an old ship's creakings,
Strain'd in a gale—you view the waves surrounding
With anxious eye—and find a leak by sounding.

* It is the *duty* of every Captain to attend to such hints as far as may lay in his power.

XXVIII.

Reader, believe me, I'm *long past my boy-age*—
Have studied mankind, since set free from school—
'Tis little things that pleasant make a voyage,
Those kind attentions which oft rest on rule—
What ev'ry gentleman of liberality
Should preach, and practise, as he would morality.

XXIX.

A good example all allow is better
Than simple precept (stale as old Bohea)
I think Commanders might uphold the letter
And spirit of good breeding more at sea:
'Twould tend to their advantage, and society,
And fortune, some well know, is *notoriety!**

XXX.

Yet men there are, who'd bring all to a level—
Themselves denied birth, breeding, riches, rank ;
Low in the world—still lower would they revel
With mean ideas, grovelling to a blank.

---

* I regret to say that Commanders do not attend to this suffi-
ciently, and *some* even *seem* pleased to hear of *fracas* among their
passengers—a very bad feeling.

Such canker'd hearts drink deep in envy's chalice,
Rating what prospers most with slanderous malice.

XXXI.

The vilest carcase that a ship can load,
Is one with spleen and envy keen at labour;
Swollen with malice, like a venom'd toad,
He spits detraction on his nearest neighbour :
Too much a coward to tell those he is baiting,
On faults, or foibles, *safely vents his prating.*

XXXII.

Fair Education, thou art life to all,
Without thee, men and brutes but little differ——
I've witness'd such as just could tell a squall,
And drink rum-grog than landsmen rather stiffer,
Fond of an idle slanderer's "*tittle tattle,*"
'Bout passengers of rank, and such "*fat cattle.*"*

---

* Never sail with any Commander who gives the least encouragement to *tittle tattle,* or who has not proper respect for sex, rank, or age.

XXXIII.

Of such take heed—a hint is quite enough,
When months at sea afford a long repentance;
A good heart sometimes pleads for manners rough,
'Gainst good intention, none can pass hard sentence.
Spruce Captains, now-a-days, may court the Graces,
Yet, some on land and sea wear *different faces.*

XXXIV.

Some, gay on shore, with countenance all brightness,
At sea grow crusty, bordering on rude;
Some, acid humours manage with adroitness;
Whilst others can't be civil if they would.
Oh, pity him, who's doom'd to meagre feeding,
Dull company, bad humour, and *worse breeding.*

XXXV.

For weeks and months pent up, condole with him
Unus'd to slender fare, and manners *Tarish*—
Biscuit, and water, maggoty, and dim—
Fowls tough—with breast-bones rather sharp and *scarish.*
So near a fit, and all so nicely treasur'd,
You'd swear each stomach had been neatly measur'd.

XXXVI.

Complaints like this, perhaps, are sometimes just;
But travellers beware, and scorn to tarnish
Fair truth—a word in jest may cause distrust,
And some I've known who tales can roundly varnish.
Sailors at times may prove unlucky planners,
I've mostly lik'd them, *barring oaths and manners.*

XXXVII.

Profit by this, then figure the reverse;
Captains there are of high and liberal polish—
Politely affable, with learn'd converse,
And some with humour, what dull *Cits* call *drollish*—
Luxuriant in style, surpassing all,
Are Indiamen from China, or Bengal!

XXXVIII.

Far at a distance they leave all behind,
For method, breeding, eating, order, sailing;
One may as well remunerate in kind
A good trait, when they catch one as a failing.
The former's pleasantest to dwell upon;
But, like musquittoes,* soon as caught, 'tis gone!

* No sooner is a musquittoe caught, than it is bruised to atoms.

XXXIX.

Not so shall this—we'll keep it, since we've caught it,
Nor in ill humour let it fly away;
"Light come, light goes," a proverb, I ne'er sought it;
But since it's come, we'll just proceed to say,
Of all the *craft*** that decorate the ocean,
An Indiaman for *fare* has *fairest* notion.

XL.

Reader, that last line was not meant for punning—
Lord Norbury and I shall ne'er agree
That *puns* are wit—though on the score of *dunning,*
The law allows that's best *done* for a fee.
Gold is a bait laid sometimes by the d—l,
So *sovereigns* may lead to *sovereign* evil!

XLI.

I don't revile it, therefore don't suppose
I'm like Saint Dunstan, fighting with temptation,
Who boldly took the *"Grim One"* by the nose—
Gold was not then his saintship's contemplation.
Few holy ones, I fear, would dread his power,
Were he to pounce *now* in a golden shower.

* A sailor's term for ships and vessels.

XLII.

This punning subject far astray would lead us,
I thought we'd been on board an India ship;
Rhyme's often fickle—let none then upbraid us,
If o'er a pun, by accident, we trip.
Bad habits turn to nature, with some nourishing,
And those who nourish *puns*, deserve a *punishing*.

XLIII.

Saving Lord *Norbury*, who, a cause to clench,
Deals *special* good ones, to dull *special* pleaders—
Delighting culprits, Counsel, Jury, Bench,
And all the *Bar*—* just *barring* losing traders,
Who feel a qualm (what Physicals call quaking)
To view on *both sides*, Counsels wise wigs shaking.

XLIV.

And well they *may*—when all's not *May* with them,
Law's trying zone hath little spring to flower;
A punning humour may prove hard to stem,
Like puny gutters swollen by a shower;

* This low play on the words and syllables, is merely put down to shew the inanity of punning. Since this was written, Lord Norbury has retired from the Bench.

XXXIX.

Not so shall this—we'll keep it, since we've caught it,
Nor in ill humour let it fly away;
"Light come, light goes," a proverb, I ne'er sought it;
But since it's come, we'll just proceed to say,
Of all the *craft** that decorate the ocean,
An Indiaman for *fare* has *fairest* notion.

XL.

Reader, that last line was not meant for punning—
Lord Norbury and I shall ne'er agree
That *puns* are wit—though on the score of *dunning*,
The law allows that's best *done* for a fee.
Gold is a bait laid sometimes by the d—l,
So *sovereigns* may lead to *sovereign* evil!

XLI.

I don't revile it, therefore don't suppose
I'm like Saint Dunstan, fighting with temptation,
Who boldly took the "*Grim One*" by the nose—
Gold was not then his saintship's contemplation.
Few holy ones, I fear, would dread his power,
Were he to pounce *now* in a golden shower.

* A sailor's term for shi

XLII.

This punning subject far astray would lead us,
I thought we'd been on board an India ship;
Rhyme's often fickle—let none then upbraid us,
If o'er a pun, by accident, we trip.
Bad habits turn to nature, with some nourishing,
And those who nourish *puns*, deserve a *punishing*.

XLIII.

Saving Lord *Norbury*, who, a cause to clench,
Deals *special* good ones, to dull *special* pleaders—
Delighting culprits, Counsel, Jury, Bench,
And all the *Bar*—* just *bar*ring losing traders,
Who feel a qualm (what Physicals call quaking)
To view on *both sides*, Counsels wise wigs shaking.

XLIV.

And well they *may*—when all's not *May* with them,
Law's trying zone hath little spring to flower;
A punning humour may prove hard to stem,
Like puny gutters swollen by a shower;

* orde and syllables, is merely put down
ing. Since this was written, Lord Nor-
tench.
to r

XXXIX.

Not so shall this—we'll keep it, since we've caught it,
Nor in ill humour let it fly away;
"Light come, light goes," a proverb, I ne'er sought it;
But since it's come, we'll just proceed to say,
Of all the *craft** that decorate the ocean,
An Indiaman for *fare* has *fairest* notion.

XL.

Reader, that last line was not meant for punning—
Lord Norbury and I shall ne'er agree
That *puns* are wit—though on the score of *dunning*,
The law allows that's best *done* for a fee.
Gold is a bait laid sometimes by the d—l,
So *sovereigns* may lead to *sovereign* evil!

XLI.

I don't revile it, therefore don't suppose
I'm like Saint Dunstan, fighting with temptation,
Who boldly took the "*Grim One*" by the nose—
Gold was not then his saintship's contemplation.
Few holy ones, I fear, would dread his power,
Were he to pounce *now* in a golden shower.

* A sailor's term for ships and vessels.

XLII.

This punning subject far astray would lead us,
I thought we'd been on board an India ship;
Rhyme's often fickle—let none then upbraid us,
If o'er a pun, by accident, we trip.
Bad habits turn to nature, with some nourishing,
And those who nourish *puns*, deserve a *punishing*.

XLIII.

Saving Lord *Norbury*, who, a cause to clench,
Deals *special* good ones, to dull *special* pleaders—
Delighting culprits, Counsel, Jury, Bench,
And all the *Bar*—* just *barring* losing traders,
Who feel a qualm (what Physicals call quaking)
To view on *both sides*, Counsels wise wigs shaking.

XLIV.

And well they *may*—when all's not *May* with them,
Law's trying zone hath little spring to flower;
A punning humour may prove hard to stem,
Like puny gutters swollen by a shower;

* This low play on the words and syllables, is merely put down to shew the inanity of punning. Since this was written, Lord Norbury has retired from the Bench.

Subsiding soon—their little depth you find,
With nought but dirty sand, or useless mud behind.

XLV.

A play on words is harmless, we'll admit—
Still must maintain (devoid of all malignity)
However folks may laugh at puns for wit,
Long robes, and wigs, suit better solemn dignity.
Puns chime not well, when culprits' chains are clanging,
Nor as accompaniments to thoughts on *hanging!*

XLVI.

There is a time for all things, but blaspheming—
Enigmas, punning, or a merry song,
May soften care, or banish senseless scheming—
All dull attendants on a voyage long.
Captains themselves may sometimes serve as riddles,
And Indiamen we know are fam'd for *fiddles!**

XLVII.

For general comfort—for a steady crew—
For plenty, regularity, and order—

* Music and dancing are generally found in Indiamen.

For good society (when there are *few)*
Society, like caps, must have its border.
'Tis out of fashion when there's much disparity,
Good breeding cannot chime with low vulgarity.

XLVIII.

Commanders, take the hint—I give it gratis;
A ship itself's a little world at sea—
Your charge is great—alas! how short ey'd Fate is,
And yours a trying, arduous destiny.
A different way you'll find in different people—
So hath each village church a different steeple.

XLIX.

Thou art a slippery article, fair Fame,
Catching the wind at times, in method rarely:
How many fortunes hail thy breath, and name,
How many fare upon thy favours sparely?
There is a star, I certainly do think it,
Of luck with mortals—*but some people blink it.*

L.

I wish that star had sooner shone on me,
A wish unstain'd by discontented whining:

What *fate ordains* must rest—so let it be—
My Autumn 's come, and roseate health declining.
With appetite too good to relish starving,
'Twas on an Indiaman I first learnt carving.

LI.

There, *Writers* and *Cadets** should volunteer,
To learn the useful science of dissecting.
Tough fowls, and ganders—trying Hodgson's beer
Between each act—nor tarts, nor pies neglecting :
Time hath its value here—no idle story—
The good things of this world are transitory !

LII.

Yet, ample credit 's due to most I've seen—
Young gentlemen *on this* use circumspection :
Not over backward—sea air 's sharp and keen,
And tarts and puddings short survive dissection.
Some seem to need, what 's very useful knowledge,
Meek, modest manners—*seldom gain'd at College.*

* If young gentlemen would commence learning to carve on
board ship, they would not *expose* their awkwardness on shore.

LIII.

Upon this topic one might much enlarge—
Parents, a hint to you's not out of season:
Pity Commanders—hard the irksome charge
Of froward girls—when deaf to sober reason.
A point may fail, through want of proper handling,
So babies fall, by awkward nurses' dandling.

LIV.

Fair ladies, joy and hope of all that's good,
Be cautious how you play the *salamander:*
Men are but mortals—ships are made of wood—
And love, like fire, may ruin a Commander.
When misses scorn advice—sage rule forsaking,
I know no better place for *sure* love making.*

LV.

Gay flirting misses soon grow proud and pettish,
When beaus of all sorts dangle in their train;
The Lord defend me from a wife coquettish,
Or *office dandies,* ugly, old, and vain.

---

* The opportunity on board ship, where people meet every day, is certain—and therefore the charge of young ladies is too often a serious one.

K

Some traits I'll tell you in a way auricular,
As facts on paper might seem *too particular*.

LVI.

Ah, many a lovely girl's youthful head
Astray is turn'd, by foolish *flirting matrons;*
Slow in belief—yet hoarding what is said,
What pleases most, they take for kindest patrons.
The dullest student's often the most pat,
And Pope's authority I quote for that.

LVII.

Like towns, ships differ, dirty, neat, or clean—
New, old, or leaky—folks with different traces
You meet, some elegant—some plain—some mean—
Some who well know, and some *do not* their places.*
One maxim I found true in every weather,
That "*impudence* and *ignorance*" go link'd together.

---

* Some of the *mates* of "*country ships*" do not appear to attend to this—and I must observe to Commanders, that it is their *duty* to have a becoming courtesy and respect paid to passengers of rank and respectability.

LVIII.

Trafalgar, since *thy* days sea themes are dull;
Yet are there captains, mates, cadets, and writers,
Who with *such hints* might decorate a skull,
However stale to *critical* inditers.
Rhyme hath its rules, though fashion sways despotic,
Dull verses sometimes prove a *good narcotic*.

LIX.

Commanders, I have felt for you ere now—
Your situations oft require adroitness;
Let different tempers ruffle not your brow;
But every act be govern'd by politeness.
I know no station that requires more management,
And this I say to nobody's disparagement.

LX.

Polite to all, fair courtesy observing,
With due attention mark sex, rank, or age;
Among your crew, encourage the deserving—
By good example petty feuds assuage.
Discountenance low scandalous delighters,
And *scorn* mean, envious, *double-fac'd backbiters*.

LXI.

There is a manner, with a wish to please,
A nicety which few at sea excel in—
Rough elements don't yield a polish'd ease,
Nor does that article in schools much dwell in.
Knowledge may spring from studying moods and tenses;
But " *common sense*" is best of all the senses.

LXII.

Caution on board a ship rests with the wise,.
Where every proper man should keep his station;
When the heart feels, there's language in the eyes,
Though mute the tongue, and foreign be the nation:
The heart will speak—but, for the sake of printing,
Reader, adieu—and profit by this *Hinting*.

RUMINATION.

I.

I LOVE to think upon the days long past,
Upon old friends, and friendships, when not jaded;
Upon past scenes, which *Lucre's* with'ring blast
Nipp'd in their bud—but never to be faded.
I love to ponder on the shores of Britain,
For there my hopes, my fears, my vows, are written.

II.

Lonely to ruminate in shelter'd grove,
O'er gurgling rill—from some romantic bower
To dwell on scenes far absent—those I love,
With whom I've pass'd the short, but happy hour—
Musing on what I've said, and still would say,
To *those* who're dearest—*but oh, far away!*

III.

In torrid regions, where *hyænas** growl,
Or prowling *jackals* chaunt their midnight glee
In hungry chorus, with the *Pariah's*† howl—
By moonlight, though my wand'rings dreary be—
Still there is pleasure in a heartfelt sigh,
For joys, alas! no more—for days gone by!

IV.

Time creeps—yet Hope, " sweet Hope," remains behind,
A balsam to the weary, though they perish:
Steadfast in Hope—serene, to fate resign'd—
Some halcyon days I still would fondly cherish.
'Tis not for self, I seize this distant cheerer—
No! 'tis for one I love—oh, far, far dearer!

V.

There's many a sea and billow rolls between—
There's many a tedious calm, and stormy sky;

* The noise of the hyæna is particularly harsh, and melancholy wild.
† The dogs of an Indian village generally howl with, or answer the cry of, jackals, which abound in most places.

There's many a rock and sand-bank lurks unseen,
And many a flash of lightning dims the eye.
There's many a chance unknown alike to any—
Days, weeks, and months to pass away—how many?

VI.

Then speed, old Time! whip on, quick fly, ye *Hours!*
Till former scenes past happiness renew;
Green fields, grey steeples, and Martello towers,
And Dover's cliffs and castle bless my view:
Ramsgate, and Deal—North Foreland's lumination,
" *Let go the anchor*"—*farewell* RUMINATION!

———o———

AN ODE,

Addressed to that source of all evil,
Cause of joy and sorrow,
Avarice and prodigality—pomp and misery—
Hope and fear—smiles and frowns—
Pride and arrogance—murder and robbery—
" Treason, stratagems, and spoils;"
Who can make great men LITTLE, *and little men* GREAT—
Thou slave of FORTUNE,

MONEY!

" In vain may heroes fight, and patriots rave,
" If secret gold sap on from knave to knave."

POPE.

PLAGUE of my life—curse of my days—

For you I've sought Sol's torrid rays;

But still for thee in vain I gaze,

Curs'd Money !

Great is thy charm to make man roam,

To quit contentment—kindred—home—

In India's clime to fret and foam,

Sad Money !

O yes ! 'tis thee the crowd adore,
Kings—Princes—Patriots—for thee roar—
E'en Poets-Laureat strive to soar . . .
                              For Money !

Bishops will preach ; and lawyers plead—
Judges pass sentence—merchants trade—
Unwilling Subs attend parade,
                              For Money !

What makes the soldier bleeding lay,
The sailor board without dismay,
And brib'd commanders run away ?
                              But Money !

What causes spendthrift heirs to rave,
At every attempt to save,
And wish fond parents in the grave ?
                              Vile Money !

For thee fair damsels feign a smile,
To gain an equipage in style ;
Yet hate thine owner all the while,
                              Base Money !

What forces beauty " YES " to say,
To hoary dotard cold as clay—
With phiz to frighten crows away ?

         'Tis Money !

Parch'd as a pea—thin as a post—
With countenance like Hamlet's ghost,
Old ladies may young lovers boast,

         For Money !

Yes ! thy d—d jingling, glitt'ring glare,
O'erturns dame nature's fost'ring care ;
And drives us mortals to despair,

         Curs'd Money !

Lovers for thee will risk their necks,
Young jockies race old spavin'd hacks :
And *paper* gamblers* aim at *lacs*.

         Of Money !

* Alluding only to such as deal largely, if not solely, in paper
currency—which *sometimes* proves no better, than French Assig-
nats in days of yore.—"*Lacs.*" A lac is 100,000.

Eager to win, though sure to lose—
Dealing in nought but I, O, U's,
Such may thy cumbrous clink abuse,

Hard Money !

Thy spleen o'erflows on Adam's sons,
You brought them tyrants—dice and guns,
And, worst of all, catchpoles and duns,

Vile Money !

Oh ! how voracious landlords swear,
And gaping waiters stand and stare,
When, bills presented, guests declare—

No Money !

Thy brazen image *Thieves* admire,
Stop man and coach, at thy desire,
With " Quick, deliver (or I'll fire)—

" Your Money !"

You make old *Cobbett* whine and rant,
The nation's poverty descant ;
'Tis *he*, not England, that's in want

Of Money !

Thy pomp and pow'r deprave men's hearts,

Hey! presto—quick—from thee up starts,

A savage race call'd *Buonapartes,**

                 Vain Money!

How many mortals for thee snivel,

Thou root of envy, sin, and evil,

Yet never think thou art the devil,

                Curs'd Money!

'Tis you make nations disagree,

Enslave men born to be free;

War and its horrors spring from thee,

                Sad Money!

Yet, after all, I needs must say,

You're a good fellow in your way,

And understand "*a rainy day,*"

                Kind Money!

So do not think I've gone too far,

But smile on me, and Mister *Star;†*

'Tis RHYME we wage, not dismal war,

                With Money!

---

* When this was written, Bounaparte was in the zenith of his glory, and had his eye upon British gold.

† This first appeared in the "*Oriental Star.*"

THE PICTURE.

I.

Give me the Girl, that's frank and free,
Whose candour shews her mind's untainted;
   As I love her, let her love me,
Unpatch'd, unspotted, and unpainted.
      Her eyes be bright,
      Her teeth be white,
Lips red as cherries, or vermillion;
      Her skin snow fair,
      With auburn hair,
She's mine! were I but worth a billion!

II.

   Let rosy cheeks in health fair glow,
An oval visage slightly languish;
   A heart that feels another's woe,
A husband's joy, content, or anguish;

Then be she young,

Her nerves well strung,

In needle-work expert and handy,

Love in her smile,

Heart free from guile,

With breath as sweet as sugar candy.

III.

In music let her taste be true,

No sing-song chorus empty jingle,

In reading she must shew it too,

Amusement with instruction mingle :

Of middle size,

But not *too wise*,

To scorn advice, or think it folly ;

In spirits high,

Ne'er heave a sigh

Oppress'd by care, or melancholy.

IV.

Be she in all things apt and fit,

Accomplish'd, yet in manner simple ;

Too wise to make *attempts* at wit,

Good natured—on each cheek a dimple.

In love with home,

Nor prone to roam,

No neighbour's fame unduly handle;

But view as small

The flaws of all,

A foe to envy, spleen, or scandal.

V.

Mild, modest, meek, in language pure,

Her words soft music, sweet as honey;

Her presence for my cares a cure—

Nor aught the worse, if she has money.

Yet if she's kind,

And to my mind,

I seek not birth, estate, or riches;

And this I'll say,

My angel may

Wear any garb, except—"*the* BREECHES!!!"

AN ENSIGN'S SOLILOQUY.

"Ne cede malis, sed contra audentior ito!"

THE noise and bustle of a camp is misery—
In torrid climes expos'd to noon-day's heat,
Say ye, who, banish'd from your native shores,
Dragging a wearied life of toil and woe,
No cheering hope to soothe a long sojourn—
Say, can a frothing glass of mellow beer,
Or gladd'ning sight of claret's roseate hue,
Should chance, which seldom comes, such kindly offer—
Say, can such chance subdue a Sub's dull cares,
By day—by night—no rest—'tis all the same—
In camp where rolling drum, and whiffling fife,
Or screaking bugle, raise their hated sounds,
The dismal howls of half-fed *Pariahs*,*
The baser tones of famish'd *Dhobies*'† asses,

* Indian dogs.
† "*Dhobie.*" A washerman.

Or shriller key of shrieking jealous wives,
Whose tongues, let loose—old Billingsgate excel.

Say, can the meagre chink of Ensign's pay,
*Sonauts** two hundred—two, and Annas six,
Make up for sleepless nights, and toilsome days,
Parboil'd to fume in one's own perspiration?
Round comes that thing yclept an 'Order Book'—
Perchance therein what seniors term a wig,
Perhaps for Picquet, or for some curs'd Guard,
Where rounds, and grand rounds, mortify the soul.
Then the grim look of some Field Officer,
Who, perch'd aloft upon a prancing steed,
Cries, Be attentive, mind at ev'ry hour
To see your sentries on their posts alert—
Patroles as usual, Sir, and nothing more!

Thus speeds old Time—begirt with sash and sword,
Moping I sit—legs cock'd upon the table—
Glass broke—a plated mug supplies its place,
Which once, in happier times, held foaming beer,
But now, alas! bears weak diluted gin.

* "*Sonauts*" are the Rupees in which the *military* are paid.

L

No Hookah's bubbling sound to chase the hours—
No! humbler me—in this strange hated land,
The dismal clouds of fusty dried cigars .
Is all I boast of in the name of smoke.
Thus duty calls—deprived of glorious fun
(Perhaps a horse-race or a match at loo,)
On Picquet forc'd to stick, I sigh alone,
Or curses mutter o'er a tough grill'd fowl!!

Better had I, in meek content at home,
Stuck to a counting-house, on stipend spare :
There, with a quill, have scribbled out the day,
The right-hand man of some old wealthy Jew : ˎ
Presented bills, and ta'en my daily round
For news to Lloyd's—peep'd in at Stock Exchange—
Once in the week, sly visited old Drury—
To Islington on Sundays quiet stray'd,
Or chance to Hampstead sought fresh country air—
Instead of doubling that billowy Cape,
Perch'd on a *bit of blood*, have doubled Hyde Park Corner.

Far, better far, than dismal midnight rounds,
O'er crags or dirt—through Nullahs, street or rain,
To the stale call of native sentinels,

Who, shock'd at every breeze, roars *" Hookum dur !"*
Give me a life of comfort—if not ease—
Free from the qualms of undigested bile,
Or sick'ning rays of mid-day torrid sun :
No dread of *Cholera*—or *hilly owl*—
Health without pills, or salts of Cheltenham.
Oh! for one look of my dear native land !
Yes, England ! if I view thee once again,
May I be ROASTED if I quit thy shores !

———0———

KALUNGA, or THE WILLOW!

Written on the Death of the late lamented
Major-General Sir Robert Rollo Gillespie, K. C. B.

"The paths of glory lead but to the grave."

GRAY.

I.

BLEAK was the morn—deep silence reign'd,
Save where the sparkling rockets fly—
The troops awake, since 'twas ordain'd,
By signal, for the brave to die.
  The word to form,
   And quickly storm,
Arous'd each soldier from his pillow,
  Soon shall the bold,
  In death lie cold,
And o'er their grave be *drooping willow*.

II.

Now, through the gloom, the cannon's roar
Was heard to crown each vivid flash;

Quick, musketry incessant pour,
Next sabres, shields, and spearsmen clash—
Soon friends and foes,
From earthly woes
Promiscuous lie, on Death's cold pillow;
Where cruel shot
Oft seals the lot
Of many a bride, to *wear the willow*.

III.

The crash is o'er—the battle done—
The bugles sound to march away;
Retreat's the word—the rising sun
May glare in vain for *victory*.
Slow march the brave,
A soldier's grave
Is honour, though the earth's his pillow;
Wail not his doom,
But let his tomb
Be deck'd with sprigs of *weeping willow*.

IV.

But, oh! what gallant corse lies there,
Grim, pale, and bloody, 'midst the dead?

In foremost ranks the first to dare,

As brave a heart as ever bled.

    The soldiers' toast,

    Their pride and boast,

No more their guide through war's red billow ;

    Sad shall the brave

    Sigh o'er his grave,

GILLESPIE* *rests beneath the willow !*

* The brave Major-General Gillespie was killed at the storm of Kalunga, in Nepaul, November 1814.

———o———

A SUMMER'S MORNING.

IN AN INDIAN TOWN.

"Olim meminisse juvabit."

VIRGIL.

FAINT yields yon pallid moon to stars more bright,
  Her setting form adorns those turrets grey ;
Sly prowling jackals scream the end of night,
  And village cocks proclaim the dawn of day.

Refreshing Zephyrs rustling Peepels* shake,
  Loquacious crows and *minas*† hail the morn—
Rous'd from their sluggish beds, scarce half awake,
  Fackeers in listless slumber sound their horn.

Where late was bustle—solemn silence reigns,
  Save where some mongrel howls in piteous yell ;
Of fish—of toddy—little trace remains,
  Though passing travellers the spot may tell.

* A tree well known in India as partaking of the aspen.
† "*Minas.*" A Mina is a very tame, sagacious bird, about the
size of a hen blackbird. There are different species of them, and
some are taught to talk.

The sober Hindoo quits his humble bed,
    For toilsome labour, ere 'tense noon-day's heat—
Goats, cows, and bullocks, leave their half-thatch'd shed,
    Lambs joyous skip, to hail a mother's bleat.

Now ruddy Phœbus paints the eastern skies,
    Bedecks with purple some far straggling cloud;
"Milk cakes!" re-echo from old women's cries—
    Hoarse Hack'ry wheels resound almost as loud.

With earthen pitchers modest females speed
    To well-known tank, or sacred river near;
Attentive school-boys, nodding as they read,
    Chalk their dull lessons free from guilty fear.

Here, listless Musselmans in circle cow'r,
    Rude jokes quick passing as their pipe goes round;
There servants met, discuss an idle hour,
    What master's thoughtless—whose the most profound.

Along bare edges of that dusty road,
    Lean, shackl'd horses seek their scanty fare;
The patient ass, that bends beneath his load,
    Would gladly stop, the meanest shred to share:

But no—those clothes must all be wash'd ere noon,
   Some bridegroom, anxious, waits their quick return—
Perhaps, some sorrowing father claims them soon,
   In best array a much-lov'd child to burn.

'Mongst yonder distant tow'rs of azure hue,
   Whence gold far shone at rise, and setting sun;
Where Princes dwelt—wild doves and pigeons coo;
   Through want of faith,* its former Lords undone.

Fair to the view, there once a palace stood,
   There pride, in grandeur, did vain state display—
Now other monarchs—tyrants of the wood—
   Amidst its ruins pass the sultry day.

Here, many a sumptuous feast—here, mirth has been—
   Health—wealth—joy—beauty—most to mortals dear;
Where crowds oft flock'd to see, and to be seen,
   No neighbouring *Ryot*,† now, dares venture near.

---

* Alluding to that want of faith and honour characteristic in the native Princes of Hindoostan.

† "*Ryot*." The lowest description of farmer.

Of sacred Mosques, whose domes majestic rose,
　Past days of splendour feeble remnants trace—
From fountains pure, no stream meand'ring flows,
　Bricks crumbling mark the desolated space.

Nor Prince, nor palace, can escape that pow'r,
　From whose sure grasp, no state—no clime is free;
Time (whose grim aspect over all doth low'r)
　Leaves nothing certain but eternity!

———o———

A SUMMER'S EVENING,

IN AN INDIAN TOWN.

A CANTATA IN TWO VOICES:

Adapted to a well known Italian air, and most humbly inscribed to the lovers of
the Sublime and Beautiful.

Viva voce!

FOAMING beer before me flowing—

Geese a gabbling—cocks a crowing—

Wind as hot as cinders blowing,

*Coolies** water busy throwing

In a *Salamander* breeze,

Tattees† only can give ease.

II.

Bus'ness for the day has ended,

Right and wrong, both well defended;

---

* "*Coolies.*" The lowest description of porters, or labourers in
India.

† "*Tattees.*" A *Tattee* consists of a frame of bamboo, filled
with the odoriferous root of an Indian grass, which is exactly fitted,
and placed at the doors or windows, and water thrown thereon con-
tinually, whilst the hot wind blows, producing a cool, refreshing
breeze.

Neighbours 'gainst each other plotting,
Black attorneys paper blotting—
Eager to find out a flaw—
Gentle Hindoos " *love the law !*"

III.

*Bundawans** now home are frothing,
All day busy—doing nothing—
Yonder jail begins a ringing,
Gentlemen and *ladies* singing;
He that steals, and pilfers most,
Is their fav'rite theme, and toast.†

IV.

Drunken rajahs' kites a flying,
Boys a running—children crying—
Women old—young men a scolding—
Pretty girls sly beholding—

---

* Native convicts, as plump (generally) as fat partridges.
† To elucidate this, it is a fact well known that convicts sentenced to seven or fourteen years' hard labour, have frequently recommenced their old trade, for the sake of good quarters, and an easy life.

Sacred paint of various dies,
Covers forehead, nose and eyes!

V.

Hack'ry bullocks' bells a jingling,
Cymbals at some marriage tingling;
Horns harsh screaking—drums a playing—
Pigs sore grunting—asses braying—
Shouts of women—men—and boys—
Making a charming Indian noise.

VI.

Pariah dogs in tuneful chorus,
Join at sunset now to bore us;
Cows and bullocks stop roads dusty,
Buggies slender—horses rusty—
Ditches deep, contain no wet—
Lord!—that gentleman's upset.

VII.

Master in the ditch a sprawling,
Stop that horse, and buggy calling,
Limping out to tell his story,
Dusty *a posteriori*—

Blacky stands and silent stares,
Careless how the carriage fares.

VIII.

Stylish Musselmans a swaggering,
Sober Hindoos homeward staggering;
From stale grog-shops, each poor body
Now retires to baung,* and toddy—
Passing time in true delight,
Sleep all day—and drink all night!

Da Capo—ad libitum.

---

* An intoxicating drug well known to most of the innocent natives!—In our town, as much ambrosial nectar can be obtained for the sixteenth part of a rupee, as will save any native gentleman the trouble of perambulation for twelve hours certain.

———o———

A CONCISE

SERIO, COMICO DESCRIPTION

OF

THE TWELVE MONTHS,

IN THE PROVINCE OF BEHAR.

Is there a day in all the year,
Too hot to drink a pot of beer?

JANUARY.

HAIL! heavenly month—the best of all the year,—
Was but each moon like thee for sport and fun,
I'd hunt all day—at eve enjoy good cheer,
Regardless of the rays of mid-day sun.

FEBRUARY.

With thee, too, February, cool and glad,
Justice I'll do thee with an honest will—
Thy days are *passable*—yet one feels sad,
To think that March succeeds thee, hotter still.

MARCH.

Yes, March, thou'rt come—and with thee flocks of quail—
  Cool are thy mornings, though thy days are warm;
O'er mango groves musquittoes' songs prevail,
  And half-fledg'd flies on windows 'gin to swarm.

APRIL.

Adieu to sport, for who can long withstand
  Sol's fiercest rays, or wind like flames of fire?
Fat ortolans may fly 'midst burning sand,—
  A book—a couch—a tattee's my desire.

MAY.

Hot is the past—yet hotter still comes May—
  Give me cool water—cold as Russian ice:
At eve, folks venture out, afraid by day,—
  So from their holes steal honest rats and mice!

JUNE.

June! thou wert ne'er an European's friend,
  Thy torrid phiz is sick'ning to the sight—
Parch'd as all feel—until thy rains descend,
  How often have I wish'd thy day was night!

JULY.

Welcome, at last, although thy phiz doth drizzle,
   Or still more gloomy clouds in torrents fall;
Few have I seen—escap'd the tongue of Grizzle—
   Six days alone—*Blue Devils* round me crawl.

AUGUST.

Avaunt, blue phantoms! cut no more dull capers—
   Pugh! rotten Indigo—by all the Nine—
'Tis good folks say to drive away the vapours,
   I'd grant it so, if *more than smell* were mine.

SEPTEMBER.

Now sacred Ganges rears his muddy head,
   Hoarse croaking bull frogs hail each passing breeze;
Poor lowland villagers great Gunda dread,
   Whilst half-drown'd tigers gladly roost on trees!

OCTOBER.

October, v rying month 'twixt calms and storms,
   O'er mud and marsh thy noon-day heat's most vile;
Death's annual friend in different modes and forms,
   Long fam'd for ague, fever, qualms, and bile.

M

NOVEMBER.

Welcome! thrice welcome—not a whit too soon,
   Late scorch'd by sun—or delug'd sore by rain:
Thy cooling zephyrs seem from heaven a boon—
   Happy are we to see thee back again.

DECEMBER.

And thou, bless'd month!—who health and vigour give,
   Mirth, dance, joy, feasting, all their charms combine;
On India's plains for ever could I live,
   Was each month's temperature all *cool as thine.*

AN ELEGY,

ON THE DEATH OF A WORTHY MASTIFF DOG.

" Virtus post funera vivit."

WHAT dismal news resounds from Pariahs' throats,
That wake, ere dawn, the farmer from his bed ?
He's *gone!* proclaims each cur, with joyous notes,
We'll fearless wag our tails, since LION'S DEAD !

Oft have we seen him, with tremendous howl,
Come scampering fierce, as tyrant grim and fell;
How sharp his bloody teeth—how hoarse each growl—
Ah, many a *Pariah's** neck and ears can tell !

Let kindred jackals, yelling, plaintive say,
(Whilst sable monkeys grin for loss of tails).
What tugs, what scars, in murtherous affray,
How many mourn grim *Lion's* teeth and nails.

* " *Pariah,*" means ' of low cast,' and is applied to dogs of the
country, of mixed or bad breed. Jackals and Pariah dogs are first
cousins.

M 2

Ye purring mousers, kittens, and tom cats,
Well might ye dread fierce *Lion's* savage jaws,
He serv'd ye as ye serve poor mice and rats,
No puss escap'd on which he laid his paws.

Honest, though rough, he quickly smelt a thief,
From duty's path ne'er swerving for a boon;
To wink at theft, he'd scorn a bit of beef,
For *Lion's growl sav'd many a silver spoon!*

Since abler poets tune a muse sublime,
To celebrate the good, the wise, the brave,
'Tis just an humble bard, in humble rhyme,
Attends on *honest* LION's early grave.

EPITAPH.

Snug rest his bones, near yonder garden wall,
A dog to foxes and grimalkins known;
Ever obedient to his master's call,
Whilst *barking Genius* mark'd him for her own.

Sharp were his teeth—his gripe the most severe—
To any Pariah's grin he'd never bend;

Of him, each mongrel stood in deadly fear,
With him no *cat* or *monkey* rank'd as *friend.*

Safe o'er his grave may *cautious jackals* creep,
And as they snuff, scream forth in hungry tones,
" Our watchful foe, in silent earth doth sleep,
" *Here, cold* and harmless *now,* rest LION's *bones!*"

———o———

A FAREWELL ADDRESS

TO THE ORIENTAL STAR.

A FRAGMENT.

ONCE more the muse—and it is but *once more*—
Compell'd to write, and give dull blockheads o'er,
Now takes a solemn yet a glad adieu
Of stupid rhymers, Mister Star, and *you*.
'Tis not in anger, but with sad regret,
To see good readers tax'd—and, reading, fret:
An Editor who aims 'bove other *hom'nes*,
Forget his motto, "MICAT INTER OMNES!"
To view a Poets' Corner lost to fame,
Supplied by witlings void of sense or shame,
Where vilest doggrel—worse than Grub Street cit—
Usurps the place of poetry and wit.

Now, grog-shop poets with low language flock—
Huzza! for Wapping, and old Shadwell dock!
Eton and Westminster, of fair renown,
Must yield to rhymers bred in Horselydown;

And for a wit, with vigour in his soul,
Match, if you can, old *Hockley in the Hole !*
Now ev'ry blockhead strives to make a pother,
And calls each bard he envies, Poet—Brother—
Seizes a quill, with addl'd braincase fir'd,
In vain, to emulate what's most admir'd ;
Greedy of praise, by copying other wits,
" As one hog lives on what another s—ts."

What 's that to you ?—if they can rightly spell ;
A newspaper, I ween, is made to sell—
What 's that to you ?—it matters not one curse,
So long as *Siccas*† jingle in your purse.
Wise readers all may gape, read, spit, and howl,
Take you the money—let them pay and growl.
Print what comes first—a fig for sense or rhyme,
Your bus'ness rests in *profit, ease, and time.*
He be your bard, who scarce the difference knows
'Twixt *Byron's* poesy and *Southey's* prose—
Who, with a genius passing true sublime,
Murders *poor* prose unknowing of his crime ;

* An obscure alley in days of yore in London—its inhabitants of the vilest description.
† " *Siccas.*" The usual Rupee current in Calcutta.

Attempting wit, but left bemir'd to roll,
To shew the meanness of a filthy scroll.

Let dunces rail and froth low spleen and spite ;
Let " *Momus*" strive, in vain, in verse to write ;
Let piddling driv'llers bellow from afar,
To fill dull columns of our Indian *Star*—
Rave on—rave on—*stale* Billingsgate invoke,
To please the printers' devils with a joke.
May ye your Editor's sad toils reward,
In rhymes as silly, as in discord hard ;
In jests unmeaning, as in words obscene,
Spite, envy, meanness, poverty, and spleen :
When such he prints, 'tis natural to stare,
To ask, " *What Editor could place such there ?*"

Truth teaches wisdom—cuffs and kicks dull dogs—
Wit fattens Editors—peas and acorns hogs :
Each has its use, and honest men well know,
" As you would reap, accordingly you sow."
But where nor wit nor sense is to be found,
Where Dulness reigns in darkness, deep, profound ;
Where publishers ne'er value sound or sense,
But deem all equal—shillings, pounds, or pence ;

Then may such printers and such poets carve
Rhymes of *their own*, nor murmur if they starve :
Who deals in little—*little* should desire,
" The labourer is worthy of his hire !"
No muse e'er flourish'd on a barren soil,
Witness poor " MOMUS," 'midst strife, dirt, and toil;
Witness a youth, amidst low worldly pains,
For wit and humour sacrificing brains :
In love with *rhyme* (how luckless to admire),
No glimmering dim of faint poetic fire ;
No feeble spark (however quick he bray)
To trudge through *Billingsgate*, and light his way.
Had his dull publisher but known to choose,
And sav'd, by *flame*, a worse than dogg'rel muse;
Then might he secretly, though sure to fail,
Aim at a hair from Pegasus' long tail :
Labour he might, like pack-horse, ass, or mule,
But all in vain—no poet's form'd *by rule.*
Types, presses, printers, *all* can never force—
What comes from nature, sticks to nature's course.

Thus have I seen two lusty awkward fellows,
Hard puffing grin, and blow a pair of bellows;

But was the task ordain'd, to save their souls,
No cheering flame raise they from earthly coals;
Harder they puff—but still 'tis waste of blast,
So curse bad bellows, and dull coals at last!

The hint is good—I give it—rather loth,
May it serve MOMUS,* and his printer both.
Better for *him*, had publishers ne'er printed,
Nor shewn how *shamefully* for rhyme they're stinted.
Let the first read—and reading rightly think,
That *poetry* rests not on *pen* and *ink*.
And may *our Editor* (with judgment wise)
Learn what to print, and fairly what despise.
May Pope's† fair lines ne'er cover dirt or spleen,
Though *wit* prove scarce, let *decency* be seen.
A lady turn'd with scorn from his door,
By words of "ugly b—ch, and wanton w—e!"
Grant him choice bards, with sense and rhyme to please,
Some traits of genius, gracefulness, and ease;

---

* "*Momus*."   At the period this was written, a stupid blockhead,
under this signature, disgraced the "*Oriental Star*" with his
scandalous puerile effusions.   The *Star* subsequently had a rapid
decline, and was reported to have committed "*Felo de se*."

† Two lines of Pope's served as a standing motto to the poetry
in the *Star*—" Ye muses ever fair and ever young," &c.

Oh, send him wisdom—(deep howe'er it lies)
To know what poet and what wit to prize.
. And should it chance (as chance perhaps it may)
Some friendly critic, in a humorous way,
Ventures advice—and he sound counsel shuns,
Hide him, ye devils, from outrageous *duns.*
May *tipstave's* paws his shoulders ne'er *caress,*
But claw his poets—ere they stop his press.
Then may a corner, now too often lost,
Be sav'd *to readers,* without let or cost—
And he by study, not professions vain,
His "MICAT INTER OMNES" pure maintain.

CONTEMPLATION !*

"Non est vivere, sed valere vita"

MARTIAL.

I.

In India's sick'ning clime, and torrid rays,
No more shall *Hope* stretch forth her fost'ring hand;
No more with rapture view my native land,
Doom'd here an *exile*, I must pass my days.

II.

Now wrinkles o'er my sun-burnt visage creep,
No work of *Time*, but grim relentless Care;
Teas'd by ill health—nigh driven to despair—
When I think on past days, Oh! I could weep.

III.

Mind ill at ease, and constitution sore,
Young still in years, yet early doom'd to fall—
(Like plant exotic nail'd against a wall)
Wither'd I pining droop, to bloom no more!

* Written during the rainy season.

IV.

What, then, are riches—what is birth or power?
Accurs'd be he who first sought care and wealth—
Give me *content*—my native clime, and health—
On others, Plutus! let thy favours shower.]

THE TRUE LOVER'S KNOT;

OR,

POOR Q.'s FINALE!

"Improbe amor quid non mortalia pectora eogis!"
VIRGIL, Æn.

I.

LISTEN, swains, unto my ditty,
  Pithy, mournful, short, and true,
Cruel Phillis, void of pity,
  Stole the tender heart of Q !

II.

Mean her person—cross'd by nature—
  Rotten teeth—and those but few;
Nose ascant, to hide each feature,
  Chin to meet—and ruin Q !

III.

Eyes at heaven and earth wide staring,
  One was white—the other blue—
Limbs that limp'd for want of pairing,
  Wrung deep sighs from amorous Q !

IV.

Camel back, waist lank, and crooked,
    Moving fast her mouth she'd screw—
Hands like crab's claws, red and hooked—
    Drum-stick arms smash'd poor Q!

V.

Hair she could not boast of any,
    Wigs she had and patches too;
Wrinkl'd forehead—freckles many—
    Lantern jaws, too much for Q!

VI.

Scraggy neck, uneven shoulders,
    Head to one side hung askew,
Frowns to terrify beholders,
    Spoke as smiles to gentle Q!

VII.

Still had she *ten thousand graces*,
    Beaux in plenty to undo;
New *yellow boys*, with shining faces,
    Touch'd the tender soul of Q!

VIII.

Will, who panted after riches,
    Soon as Madam's charms he knew,
With-jockey frock—black satin breeches,
    Ruinated Mister Q !

IX.

Like a " *true lover* "—life low scorning,
    Silken garters, edg'd with blue,
One dismal, rainy, Sunday morning,
    Stopp'd the windpipe of poor Q !

X.

Lovers all, beware of guineas,
    Hide your garters when ye woo,
Leave silken knots to simple ninnies,
    Warning take from *dangling Q !**

* This was written in consequence of a love-sick swain having
sent some puerile rhymes to the " Oriental Star," under the signature of Q.

AN ODE TO GIN.*

"Festina lente."

COME to my aid, repeller of sad care,
Hail! friendly spirit, who doth most excel—
Ah, oft's the time thou'st nail'd me to my chair,
For long I've known thee, and have *lov'd thee well!*

When sad reflection, with her gloomy train,
And midnight revel struck remorse, dismay—
Relief from *thee* I never sought in vain,
Thy potent pow'r dispell'd ill luck at play.

O'ercome *by thee,* amidst the *Coal-hole's†* din,
Oft have I strove in vain to find the door—

---

* I hope my readers will pardon the vulgarity of the liquor, and consider it a bottle of Charles Wright's best sparkling Five-and-sixpenny.

† "*The Coal-hole.*"—This is a noted place in the Strand where curiosity attracts an assemblage of all sorts of people—especially to see and hear certain *actors,* who are used to assemble here on *Saturdays,* Mr. Kean as I have heard among the number, and there, *spouting, singing* and *swigging,* are the order of the evening, and sometimes very good.

N

And more than once (I blush for thee, O gin!)
Thou'st laid me senseless, sprawling on the floor.

Yet, thou wert kind—for though I've slept on stones,
Sometimes in alleys, and in dewy air—
I ne'er till now complain'd of aching bones,
Nor snarl'd at thee, although thou laid'st me there.

Yes, *Gin, I love thee*—yet must speak what's true—
Thou wert not made for man inclin'd to roam;
How I've gone out when sober, well I knew;
But could not tell for *thee, how I came home.*

Still I forgave thee, clearest, purest Gin,
Though at thy name my wife would rant and scold,
If she must prate, and bellow, I will *grin,*
For prim'd *by thee,* one's heart feels wondrous bold.

Thy *spirit, pure,* may *Methodists* admire,
About how much can lighten a man's skull,
Philosophers their brains need never tire,
For well I know, that water makes thee dull!

Wise ones avow, thou mak'st folks double see,
Hiccup, and stagger, sore inclin'd to fall—

On abstruse topics we'll ne'er disagree,
Since with thee sometimes *I can't see at all!*

In days of yore—(how nimbly grey Time flies!)
My good aunt Bridget, with a look demure,
Would take her glass—then turning up her eyes,
Cry "*Ned*, my darling, *Gin's a cholic cure.*"

Ah, Gin! thou azure cordial, why rehearse
In feeble numbers thy all-matchless skill?
Truth may be told of thee in humble verse,
Thy spirit's sure to quickly cure, or KILL!

———o———

FIVE YEARS MORE.

INSCRIBED TO AN OLD BACHELOR.

"Sed fugit, interea fugit, irreparabile tempus."

VIRGIL.

ANXIOUS to hold their tenement of clay,
How many hail unmov'd the parting day;
How few are those who dream of troubles sore,
But what would banish *Death* for *one day more!*

Short as life is, 'tis open'd first with tears,
Man when he's born vociferates his fears.
Five is the age, when boys first think of *birch*,
At *Ten* thumps, baubles, grammar, school and church:
Now *Fifteen* comes, what *man* can relish blows?
At *Twenty*, "dem me"—stylish gait, and clothes.
At *Five-and-twenty*, bucks frisk, sport, and riot,
Thirty's an age when sober folks are quiet:
Past *Thirty-five*, I smoke, or relish snuff,
At *Forty*, think a pint of wine's enough.
Past *Forty-five*, I for my *jazy* call,
At *Fifty*, ride for health—but dread a squall.

When *Fifty-five*, forego all worldly strife,
At *Sixty*, think of wedding—ah ! *for life !*
At *Sixty-five*, the girls still say I'm young,
Past *Seventy*, I believe each flattering tongue.
Now *Seventy-five*, asthmatic sighs claim breath,
At *Eighty*, looking sharp at sound of *Death !*
Scarce *Eighty-five*, begin to think I'm old,
At *Ninety*, die, and now my tale is told.
Yet, passing strange, I thought I still might thrive,
To marry some gay lass at *Ninety-five !*
Wedlock enjoy'd, when verging on *Five Score*,
Had *cruel Death* but waited—FIVE YEARS MORE !

——o——

INDIGO PLANTER'S PRAYER.

Found at the bottom of an old Indigo Chest, and supposed to have
been written about the year 1810.

O Lord, deliver us from evil,
Send Buonaparte unto the *D—l !*
Let him on cinders burning roast,
Or for grim Satan make a toast.
This Corsican for brimstone made,*
Has ruin'd many a thriving trade.
Relieve *me* further from all pain,
By granting daily show'rs of rain;
So may the plant with vigour rise,
Goodly in colour, as in size;
And I full soon commence my labour;
But *not one drop* allow my neighbour.
Let him cry out—and crying want,
'Till drought has wither'd half his plant.
If further still may I request,
Let cows and horses eat the rest—
And more—should all this chance to fail—
Send him large insects, wind, and hail.

* Alluding to his taste for gunpowder.

Grant that *his* bullocks may get the rot,

And all *his Ryots** go to pot—

That walls may fall to break *his* coppers,†

And lightning fire all the choppers.‡

Let what he makes prove nasty stuff,

And very little be enough—

So bad—when people come to try it,

No honest man would dare to buy it.

A devil of a trade we'll drive,

If ev'ry Planter chance to thrive;

No purchasers I fear be found,

At two-and-sixpence in the pound;

As people say, though much I doubt it,

These fiddling Frenchmen do without it.

Whether or no—I dare presume

We'll make much more than they consume—

And as in schools 'tis understood,

" *That partial evil's general good*''—

So let *one half* of Planters fail,

To keep the *other half* from jail.

May all *my* labour—all *my* fears—

Last at the most but *seven years.*

Then grant not much—I ask no more,

Than just a quarter of a - - - CRORE !§

* " *Ryots.*"   Under farmers.   † Boilers.
‡ Sheds with thatched roofs.
§ "*Quarter of a Crore.*"   Equal to £250,000.

IRISH COURTSHIP;

OR,

PADDY O'BLAZE.

———

THE Muse that is tir'd of singing of wars,
Of Kings and of Emperors' squabbles and jars,
May find sweeter food to adorn her lays
About Judy Maguire and *Paddy O'Blaze.*

Our Pat was well known at the turf-cutting trade;
In Lim'rick, Miss Judy had serv'd chambermaid;
One night at a wake she attracted the gaze
Of slip-shodded, whiskey-fac'd, *Paddy O'Blaze.*

Poor Pat by sly Cupid was smote at first sight,
Made his bow to the damsel with speech quite polite;
Will you foot it, Miss Judy? No—I've not got my stays;
No matter—we'll jig it, said *Paddy O'Blaze.*

The pipers attentive appear'd at the door,
Whilst this pretty couple stood up on the floor—

"Arrah, what shall it be now?"—"Och! just what you
      plase—"
"Give us *Cheelun O'Guiry*—" roars *Paddy O'Blaze*.

So they tramp'd, and they pranc'd, till the pipers were
      tir'd,
And all but the *corpse** this fair couple admir'd;
Whilst Judy lamented the heat of the days,
"Take a drap o' the cratur," says *Paddy O'Blaze*.

With whiskey inspired bold Patrick grew kind,
And would be after telling a bit of his mind;
Whilst he utter'd (poor Judy blush'd all in amaze)
"My jewel, take pity on *Paddy O'Blaze!*"

"O listen, fair maid, sure I'm not to be hated,
"Since that *purty* face has poor Pat *ruinated*—
"Your black shining eyes beat the Sun's brightest rays,
"They have melted the liver of *Paddy O'Blaze*.

"My father is ould, though his *trotters* are strong,
"And mother, poor cratur, can't live over long; ·

* To such as have never seen an Irish wake this may appear exaggeration—but those who have, know that festivity and dancing
are most frequently the order of the night.

" Their *fortin*, since whiskey must shorten their days,
" Will grace, my sweet Judy, your *Paddy O'Blaze.*

" Two pigs—a blind horse—a sledge car—an ould cow—
" A garden for *pratties*—a harrow, and plough ;
" A turf stack, some shiners—*all*, Murphy here says,
" Must comfort their dearest joy, *Paddy O'Blaze.*"

Then seizing her hand—if she'd be his wife,
He swore he would love her far longer than life,
She modest replied—" *Arrah*, honey, *don't taze*,
" Och ! can't you *be asy* now, *Paddy O'Blaze.*"

But Patrick resolv'd to stick close to her side,
Until she consented to be his dear bride ;
To church soon they jogg'd, in O'Regan's back chaise,
Where Miss Judy was buckl'd to *Paddy O'Blaze.*

Returning post haste the old Hackney broke down,
Pat's broad face was cut—Judy tore her new gown ;
" Bad luck to the *Garvans*—I'll trudge at my ase
" *The next time I'm married*"—cried *Paddy O'Blaze.*

EPIGRAMS.

An Epigrammatic Prayer, dedicated to the Service of Indigo Planters.

"Fortuna multis dat minium, nulli satis."*

MARTIAL.

RAIN! send us rain—some Planters piteous call—
It comes—too much—this flood will drown us all!
Sun's next the wish—nor long we pray in vain—
It shines—is curst—and then the cry is rain.
Again rain show'rs—again for sun we pant—
Nor modest, ask *at once* for what *we want*.
Great Jove, take pity—please us or we'll scold,
The wish'd-for shower, is a—SHOWER OF GOLD.

The Origin of Punsters.

OLD Jove one day, when in a sulky fit,
Created Punsters as a curse to wit;

* Thus translated:
    Dame Fortune gives too much to many,
    Yet, never smiles enough on any.

"Wretches," he cried, "begone from hence and nibble,
"Shun wit and sense, catch words, and on them quibble."
To earth they came, as 'twas ordain'd by fate,
To *snap at words*, as *minnows* do at bait!

On a stiff Society.

DULL now I pass the days,
  We've neither mirth, nor Cupid;
But people just as grave
  And proud, as they are stupid!

Translated from the FRENCH.

WHEN he was my lover, how happy was I?
But now he's my husband—*I'm ready to cry!*

On M. NECKER—from the FRENCH.

A STOCK-JOBBER expert and bold,
  A minister half taught—
From out of *nothing* he made gold,
  And of a kingdom *nought!*

On Mr. DIMOND, author of several Dramatic Pieces.

DID the genius of *Dimond* keep pace with his *name*,
His works might ascend to the Temple of Fame;
But alas! though he glitters, 'tis like a known fly,
That lives for an hour, then sparkles—*to die!*

On a very ugly Man.

WHEN through our village gay Sir Tristram rides,
. The farmers smiling gladly wish good morn,
And cry, " God bless his Honour's phiz and sides,
  " The *crows* to-day *will spare our fruit and corn!*"

Cause for Grief.

FOR shame—why shed that boyish tear,
  Or like a child keep frothing—
Oh, my poor aunt!—(my grief's sincere)—
  Is dead—but left me - - - NOTHING!

An Indigo Planter's Definition of Wit.

LET poets twist epigrams—squabble for bays,
And rhyme forth dull ditties to pass forth dull days—
The best of the herd but a vain hope pursue,
They think wit's in rhyme—but true wit's in TRUE BLUE.

EPITAPHS.

On a Gourmand.

WHOEVER passeth by this stone,
Know that George D——— lies here alone;
No more he'll eat roast beef and humps,
For Death has knock'd him off his stumps.

On a Drunkard.

READER, whene'er this stone you pass,
Think of a bottle and a glass;
Since he whose loss we new deplore,
Most surely thought of *nothing more!*

Another.

HERE rests a man, if true what's told,
Ne'er felt the pangs of bitter cold,
Ne'er knew the want of meat, though *thirst,*
Made cruel *Death* cry, " *Stop—you'll burst!*"

On my old friend, WILLIAM W———.

HERE poor Will lies, as we all must,
Sooner or later, night or day;

Will never thought o' "*dust to dust,*"
Whilst aught he had to *wet his clay!*

On a Miser.

HERE F——r lies—no flesh—all bone—
His spirit too—for he had none;
Snug lodg'd beneath this humble sod,
For *money* was *his only God!*

On Corruption.

THE man is dead, his body rotten,
His spirit fled, and he forgotten.
Satan, take care and have *your due;*
For here he brib'd—so may he *you!*

On a Satirist.

J——s——N lies here—so pray be civil,
He's gone to ridicule the *D——l!*

On a Censorious Wretch.

HERE rests a man who, when alive,
Could never speak of any well;
Happy for us, he's ta'en a dive
To *scandalize* old Nick in h——ll!

On a talkative Friend, with an excellent Memory.

HERE E——g rests—give ev'ry man his due,

Forget not him, for he'll remember you ;

Whate'er he read on earth of man or madam,

Was ne'er forgotten since the days of Adam :

And now he's gone, if Fame doth rightly tell,

To pick an anecdote or two in h——ll !

But soon he'll soar, whilst angels round him glisten,

And cry, Here's E——g—*let us sit, and listen !*

On an old Servant.

UNDER this stone Jack R——d doth lie,

   Releas'd from worldly care and sorrow ;

And who now knows but you or I

   May lay our heads like his to-morrow.

On poor Basto ! a favorite Pointer.

HERE *Basto* lies, obedient, staunch, and true,

Four legs he had, and if worth has it's due,

A better dog than *some* who *walk on two !*

Finis.

J. GAMBLE, Printer, Mortlake, Surry.

CPSIA information can be obtained at www.ICGtesting.com
Printed in the USA
BVOW04s1017060814

361905BV00021B/471/P

9 781287 903871